# LEGACY & LOVE

# The Meditative Men Collection

by Harmony N. Soul

© 2023 by Harmony N. Soul. All rights reserved.

No part of this publication may be reproduced, distributed, or transmitted in any form or by any means, including photocopying, recording, or other electronic or mechanical methods, without the prior written permission of the publisher, except in the case of brief quotations embodied in critical reviews and certain other noncommercial uses permitted by copyright law.

Published by Invest and Indulge, LLC

ISBN: 979-8-8667-7708-2

Cover & Book Design by Harmony N. Soul

Title: Legacy & Love: The Meditative Men Collection / Harmony N. Soul

Printed in the United States of America

First Edition

This book is published by Invest and Indulge, LLC, and is sold with the understanding that the publisher and the author are not providing professional advice of any kind. If expert assistance or counseling is needed, the services of a competent professional should be sought.

The author and publisher specifically disclaim any liability, loss, or risk, personal or otherwise, which is incurred as a consequence, directly or indirectly, of the application and use of any of the contents of this book.

The images contained within this book are artistic representations and are not intended to reflect or portray any particular culture or individual. They are designed for the enjoyment and personal reflection of the reader, and any resemblance to specific persons, living or dead, or to cultural practices, is entirely coincidental and unintentional.

The application of protocols and information in this book is the choice of each reader, who assumes full responsibility for their understandings, interpretations, and results. The author and publisher assume no responsibility for the actions or choices of any reader.

First Printing, November 2023

# Author's Note

Welcome to "Legacy & Love: The Meditative Men Collection," a canvas on which your intimate reflections on legacy and love can take form. My name is Harmony N. Soul, and I've created this book as an invitation to explore the dance between the enduring impact we wish to leave and the intimate connections that color our lives.

As an introvert, I've always found peace in quiet moments, with pencils or coloring tools and a blank page. I've often discovered what's most true about myself in this silent dialogue between heart and hand.

This book is not just a series of images but a collection of prompts and possibilities, each crafted to guide you through the shades of your aspirations and the palette of your emotions. May your journey through these pages be as revealing and fulfilling as the act of creating them has been for me.

*Harmony*

# Introduction

In the rapid pace of today's world, 'Legacy & Love' emerges as a sanctuary of creativity and mindfulness. More than just a coloring book, it is a journey into self-reflection and connection. Divided into two compelling themes—'Legacy,' with imagery of young Black men prompting reflections on life's impact, and 'Love,' celebrating intimate relationships through the portrayal of Black couples—this collection invites you to slow down and engage deeply.

The unique designs of AI-generated images, featuring organic lines and minimal shading, transforms each page into a mindful experiment. Embrace this book as your Coloring Vision Board, a space where intentional coloring meets the manifestation of your aspirations in legacy and love.

May 'Legacy & Love' offer you solace, inspiration, and a pause from life's hustle, encouraging you to explore the art within and bring beauty to the world through each mindful stroke and reflective moment.

As you start this journey, let the act of coloring be your anchor and your compass.

# Mindful Coloring Tips

**Embrace Your Creative Journey**

Welcome to 'Legacy & Love,' a unique coloring adventure. If you're feeling overwhelmed, remember: this is your journey, and there's no wrong way to embark on it. Coloring is about self-expression and mindfulness, not perfection.

**Start Small, Dream Big**

- Take a moment to connect with the image. Let it speak to you.
- Choose a section that draws you in. Focus on coloring just that area to start.
- Break the image into manageable parts. Enjoy the process, one section at a time.

**There Are No Mistakes, Only Discoveries**

- Every color you choose is a reflection of your mood and perspective. Trust your instincts.
- If you're unsure, start with your favorite colors. There's comfort in the familiar.
- Remember, every stroke is a step on your creative path.

**Experiment and Explore**

- Mix and match tools. Pencils, crayons, or even markers—each brings its own texture and feel.
- Don't be afraid to blend colors or try new techniques. This is your canvas to explore; there are blank pages to practice on at the back of the book.
- Each page is a new opportunity to discover more about yourself and your art.

**Breathe and Be Present**

- With each breath, let go of fear and doubt. Allow yourself to be in the moment.
- Your coloring journey mirrors life's journey: unpredictable, colorful, and uniquely yours.

Remember that you aren't just filling in a design as you color. You're embarking on a meditative practice to connect with your inner self. Let 'Legacy & Love' be a safe space for your creativity to flourish and to exercise self-compassion as you face new challenges.

# LEGACY

# LEGACY

# LEGACY

# LEGACY

# LEGACY

# LEGACY

# LEGACY

Embrace the power and depth of your legacy. Remember, what you leave behind isn't just the tangible but also the invisible threads of influence and inspiration that weave through the fabric of time.

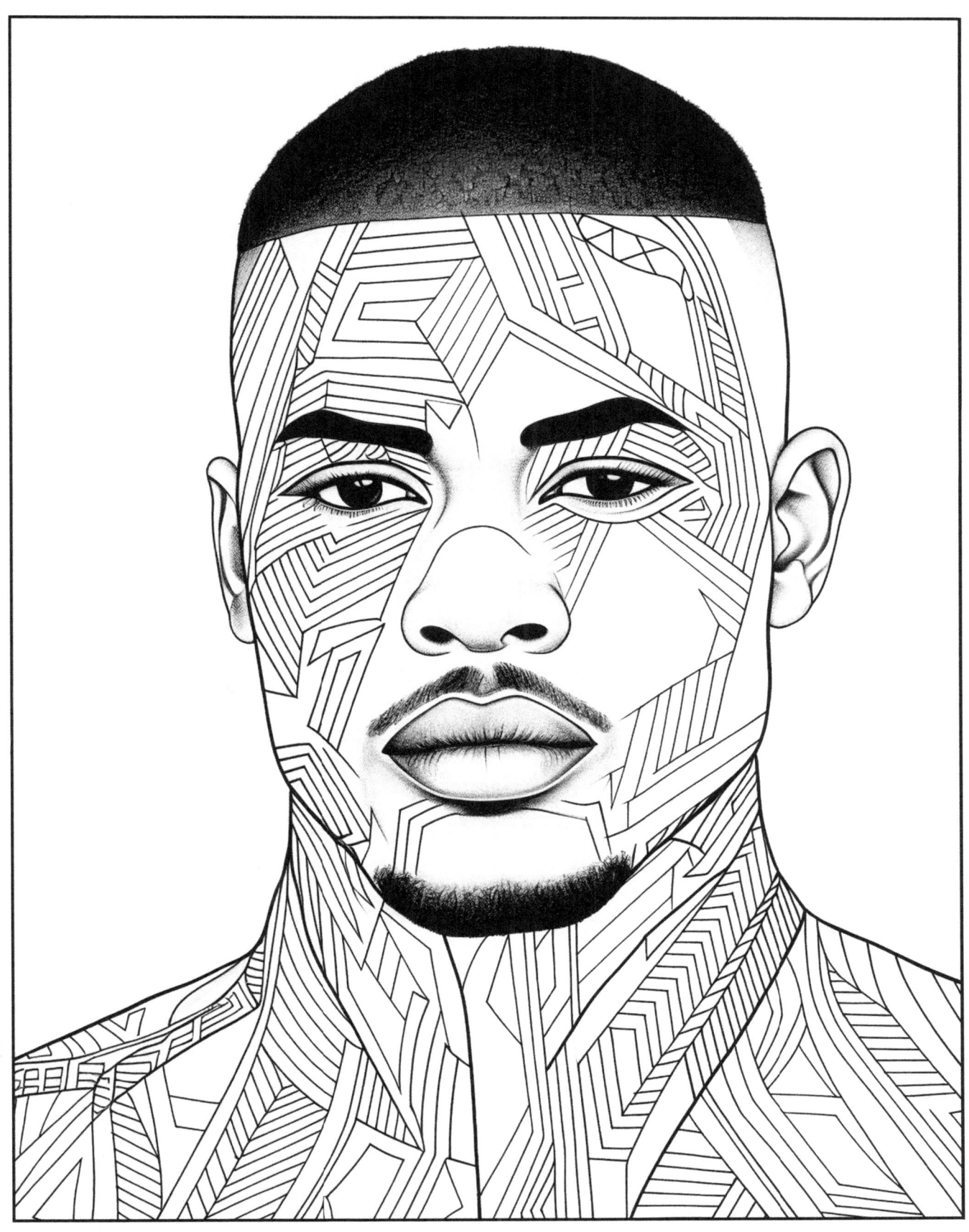

Within the lines of this image lies a pattern of potential—your potential. As you color, think about the patterns of life you're creating for those who follow.

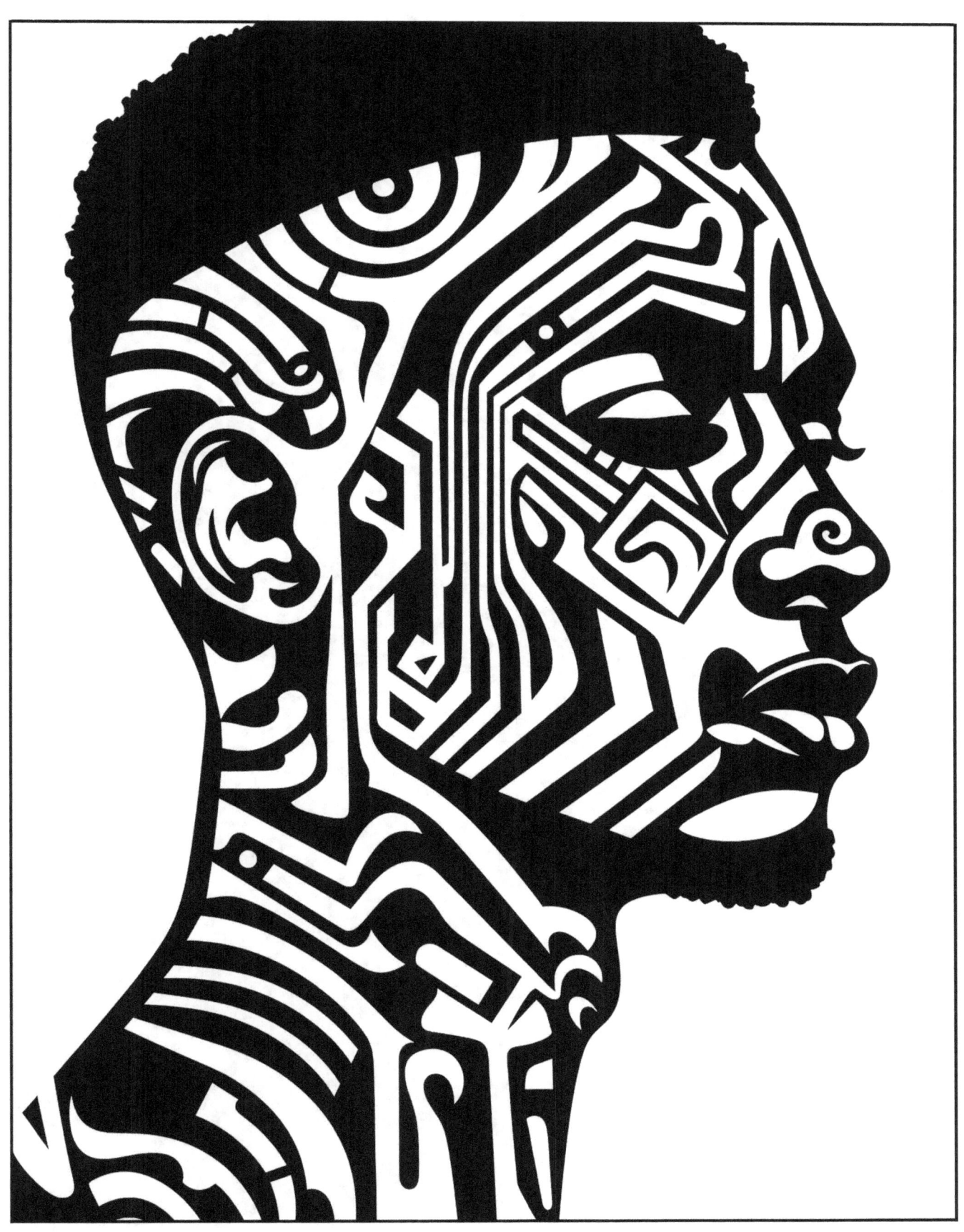

Color in the shapes that resonate with your spirit. Imagine these shapes are the foundations of the legacy you're building. How will you shape these foundations in the real world?

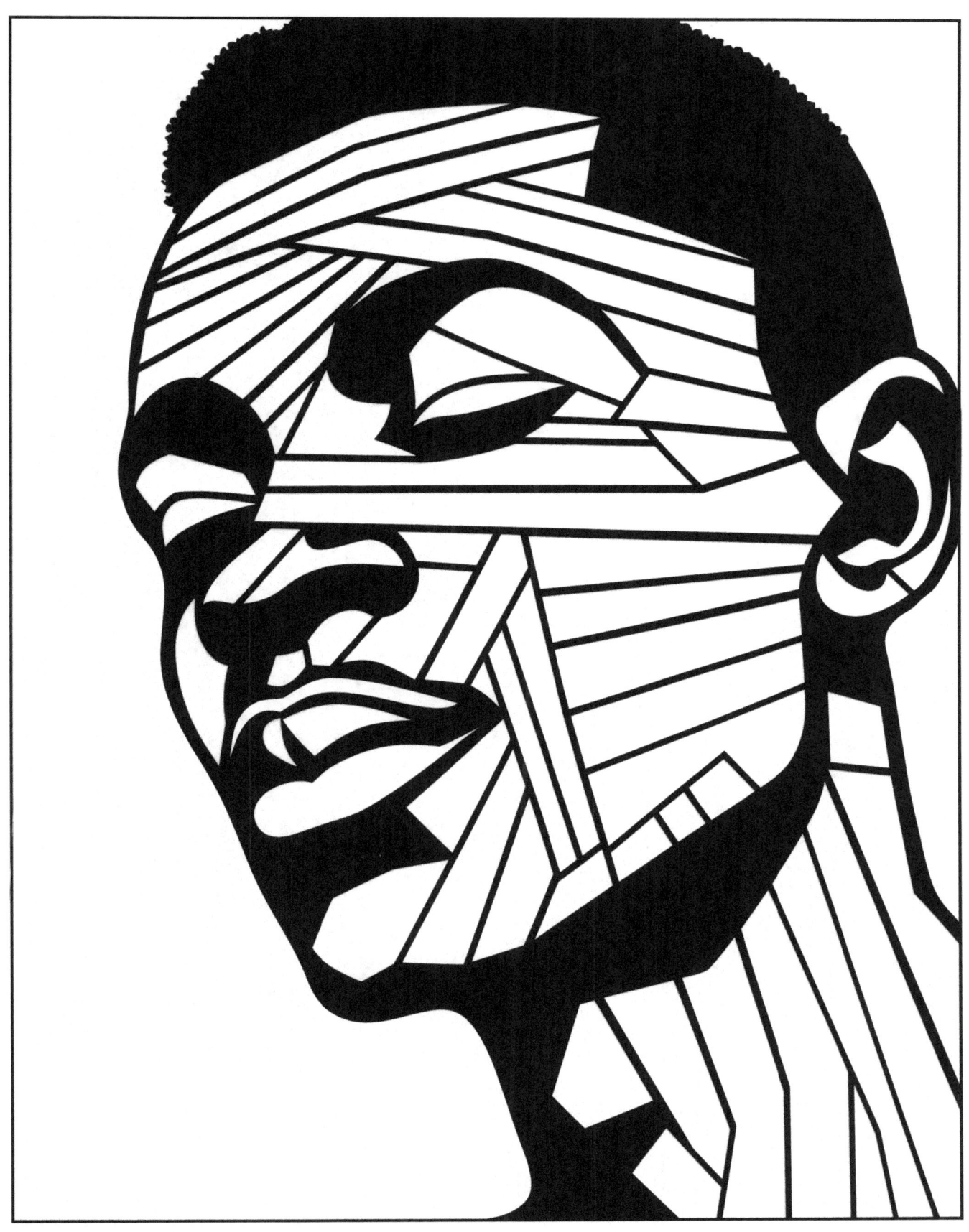

Consider the legacy of your words as you shade inside the lines. What messages do you wish to color the world with long after you're gone?

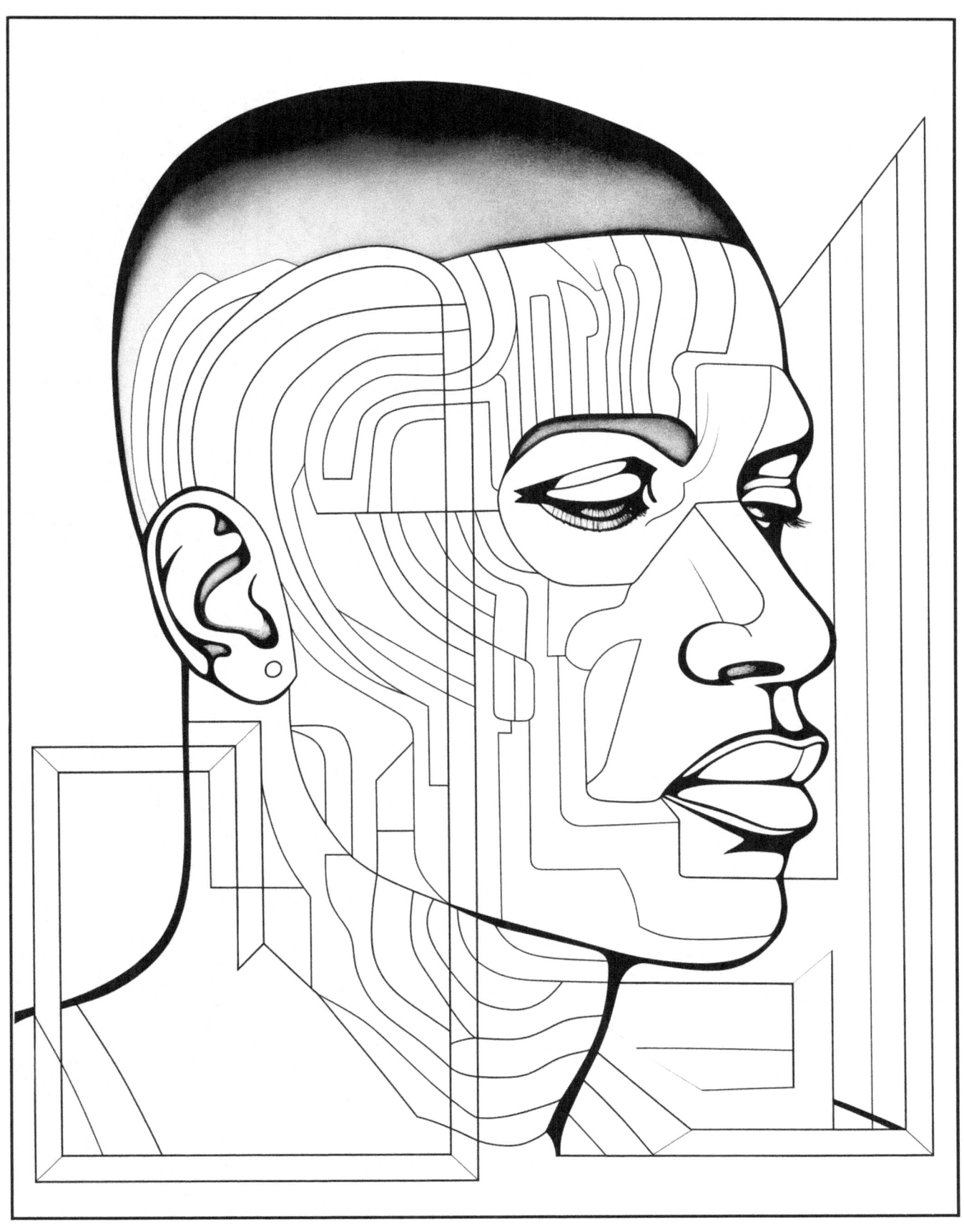

Think of a tradition that you would like to begin, one that could carry your essence into the future. What is its first ritual?

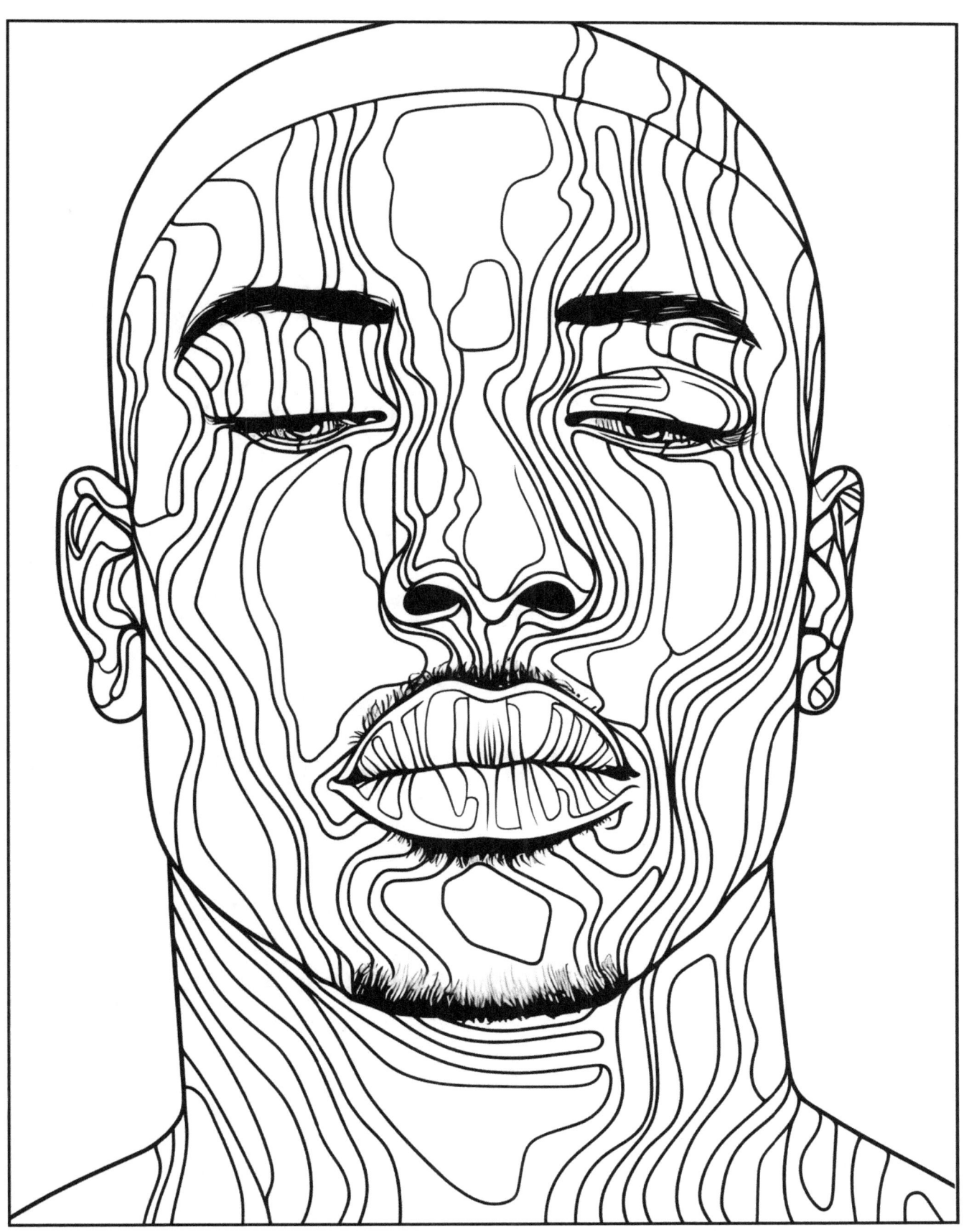

As you blend colors, think of the blend of ideas and wisdom you want to leave for the next generation. How can you start integrating these into your legacy today?

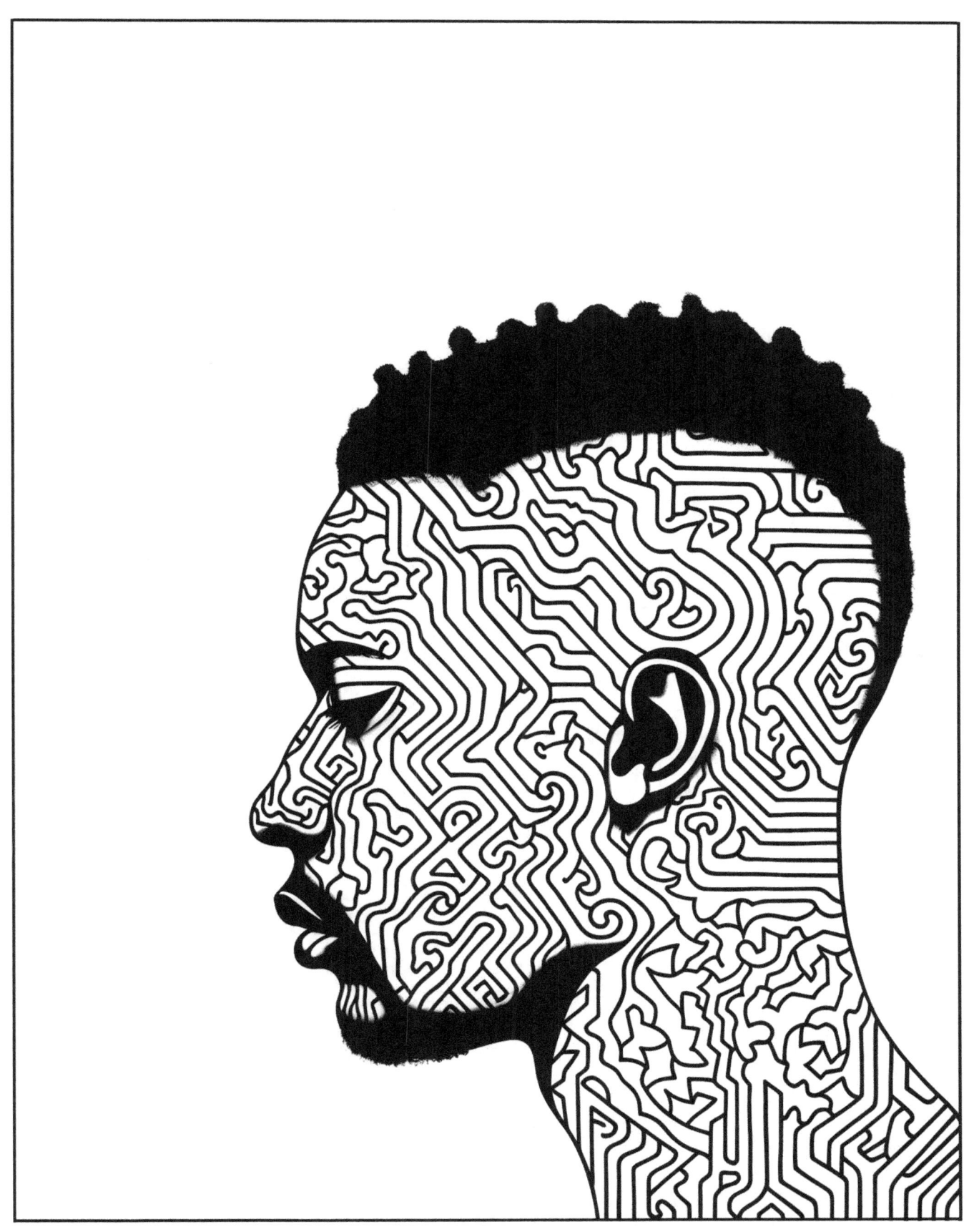

Let the act of coloring be meditative, a silent conversation with the future. How will you color the world differently with the legacy you build?

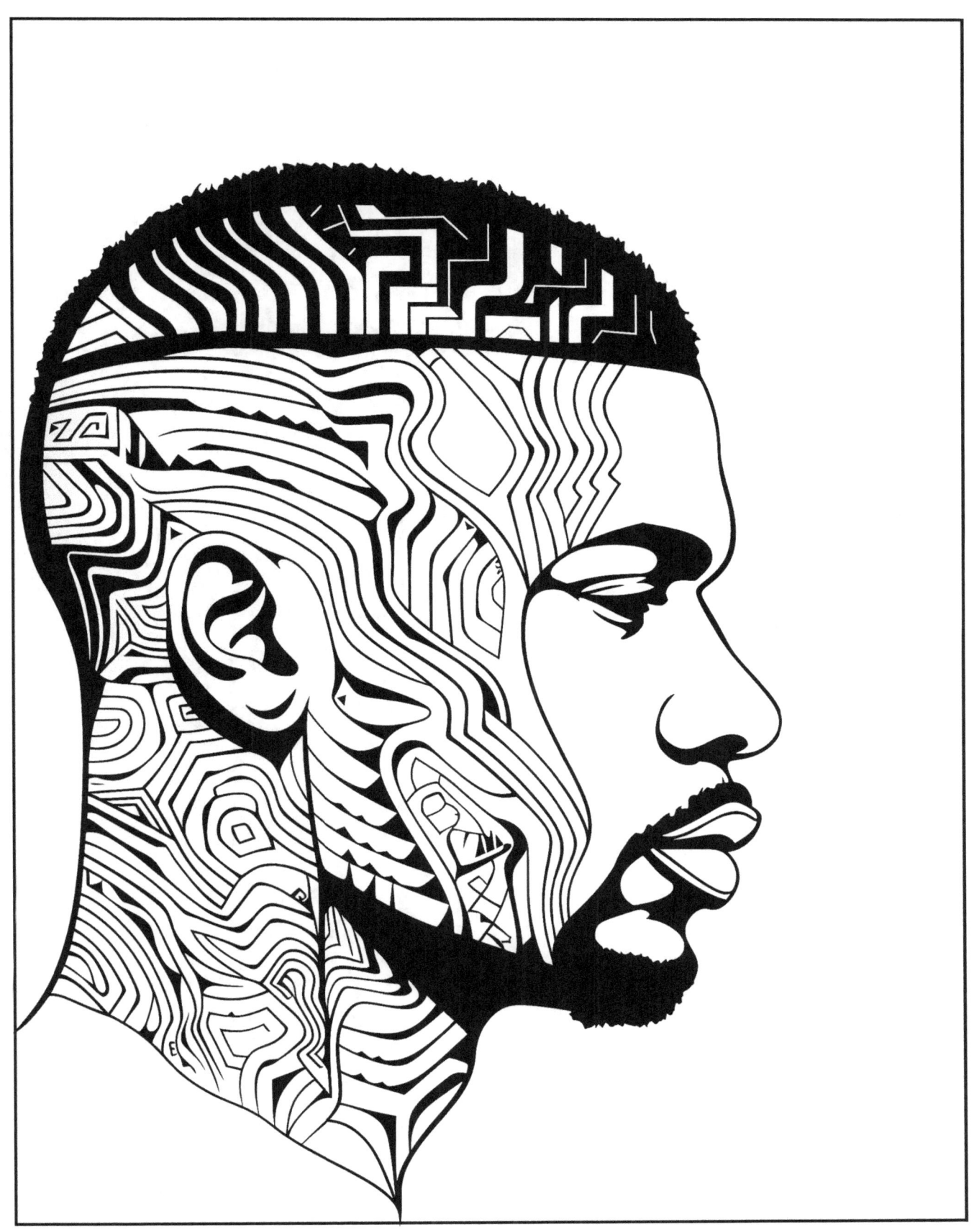

The colors you choose echo the memories you leave; with each area you fill, consider the impact of your deeds. What color will your kindness leave in others' minds?

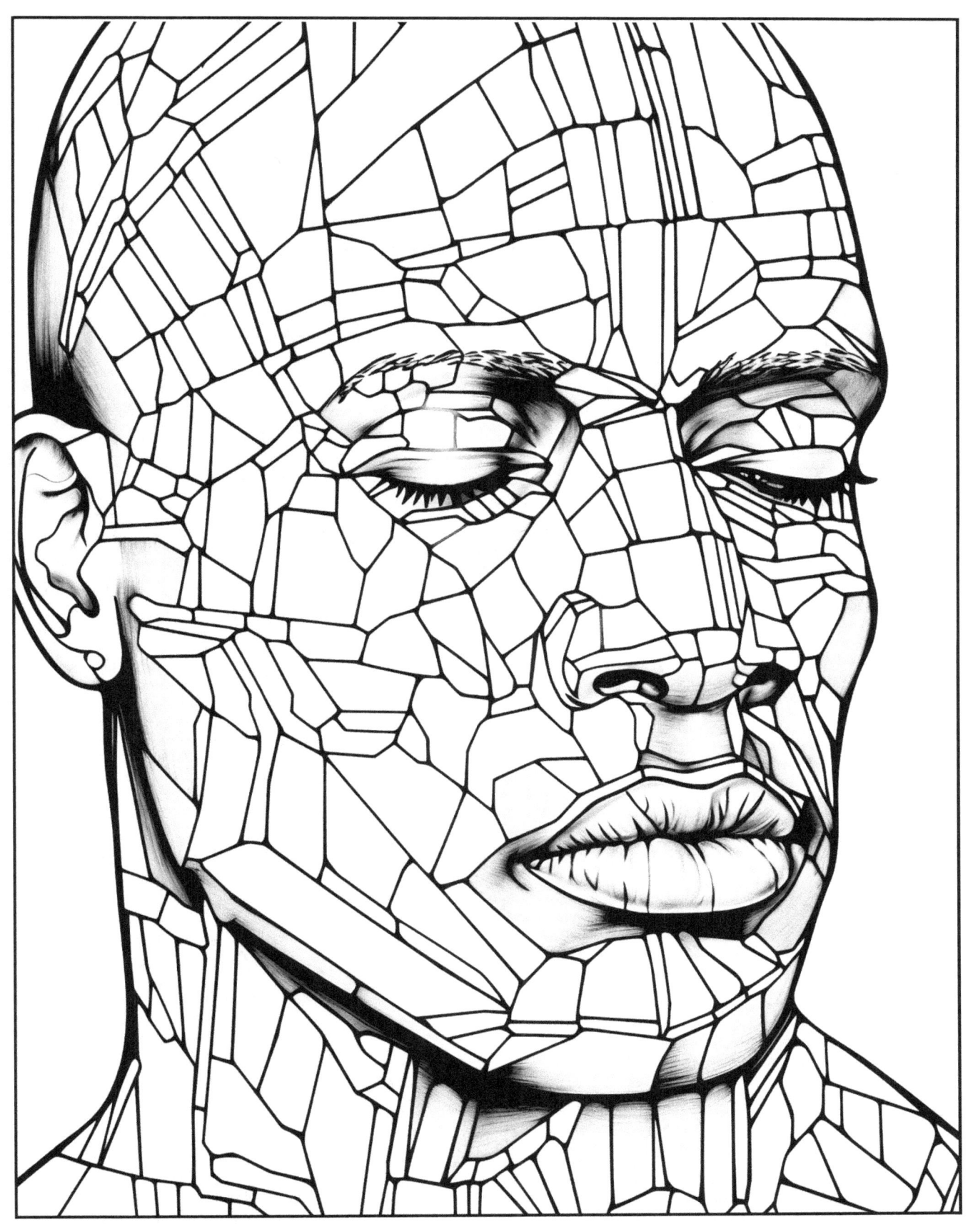

Let your palette illustrate the legacy you wish to create. What colors do you choose to paint the story of your life's work?

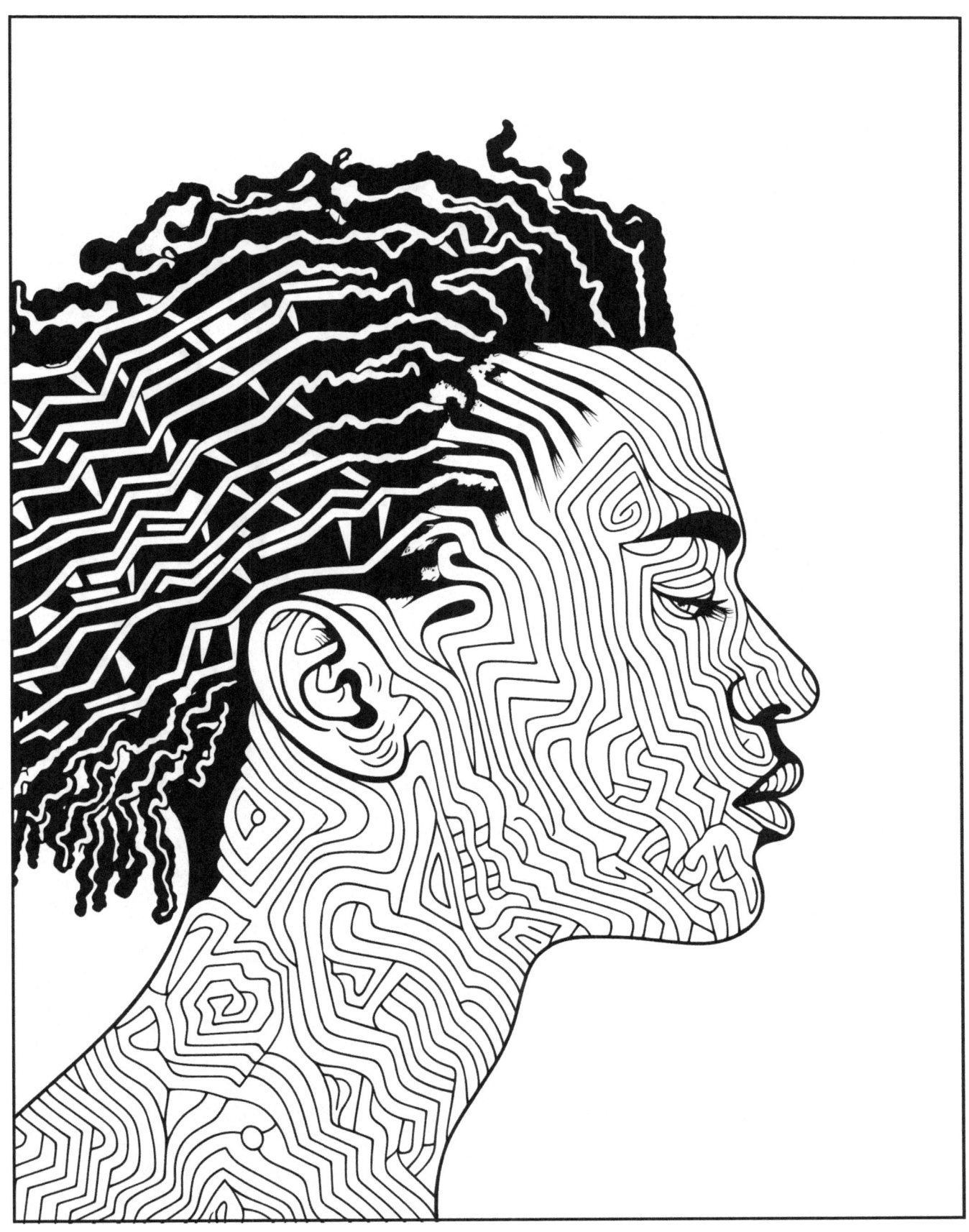

Color slowly, with intention, as each stroke represents a step towards the future.
How will your actions today color the legacy you leave tomorrow?

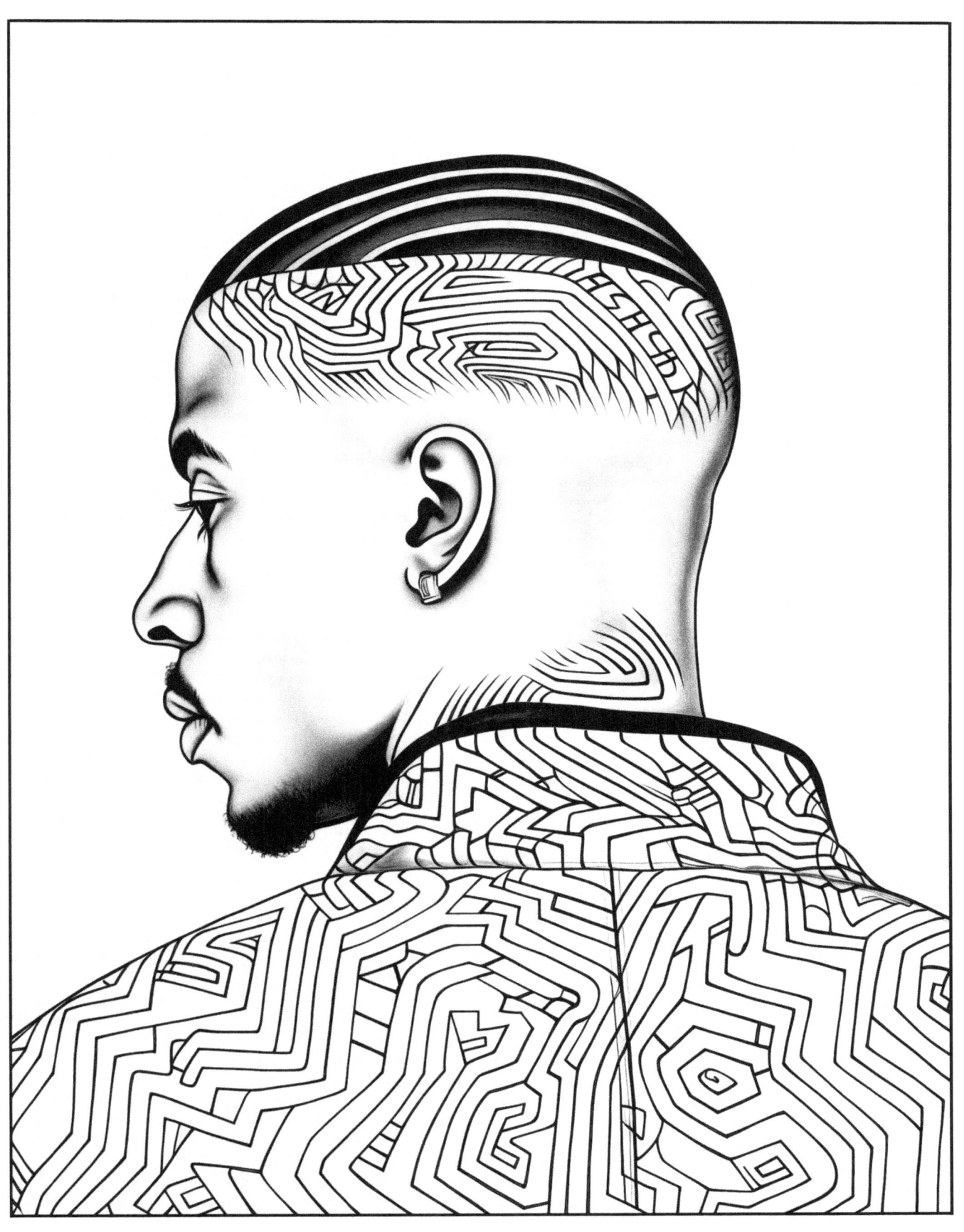

With each color you choose, envision a trait you want to be remembered for. How can you live out this color, this trait, more vibrantly each day?

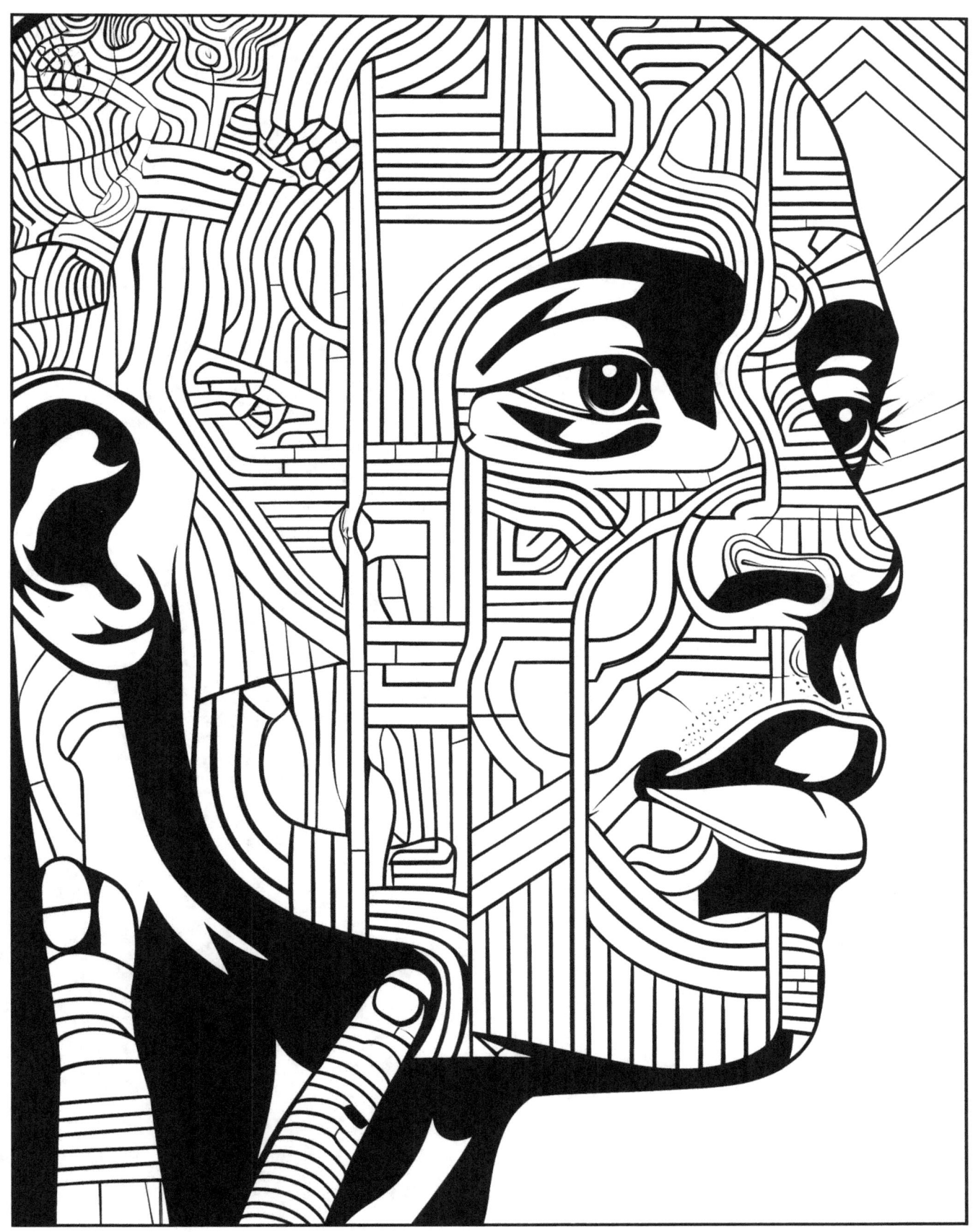

Highlight the parts of the image that stand out to you most. In the same way, highlight the parts of your character that you want to stand out in your legacy.

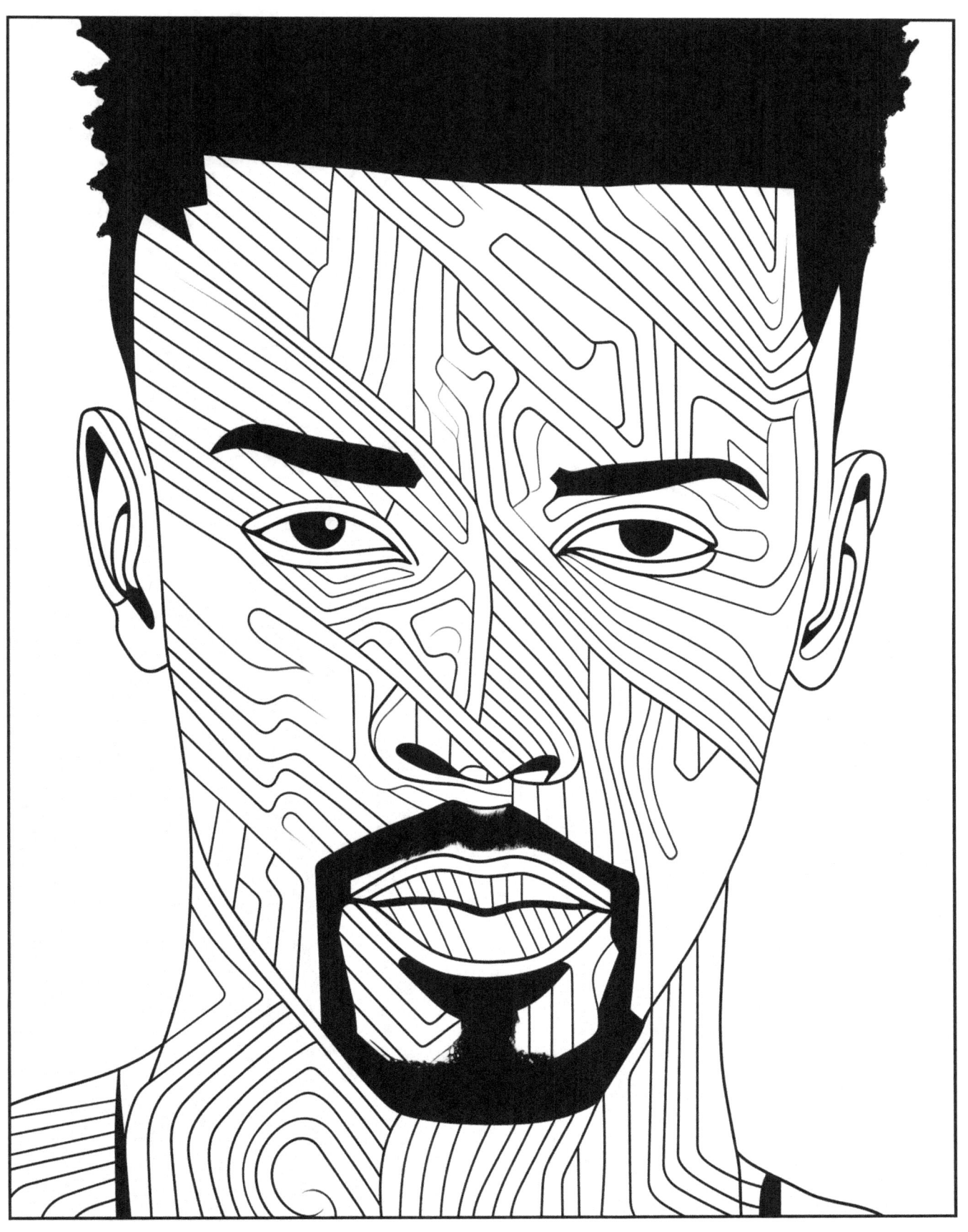

As you color, plan actions you can take to craft a legacy that endures. What are these actions, and how can you begin?

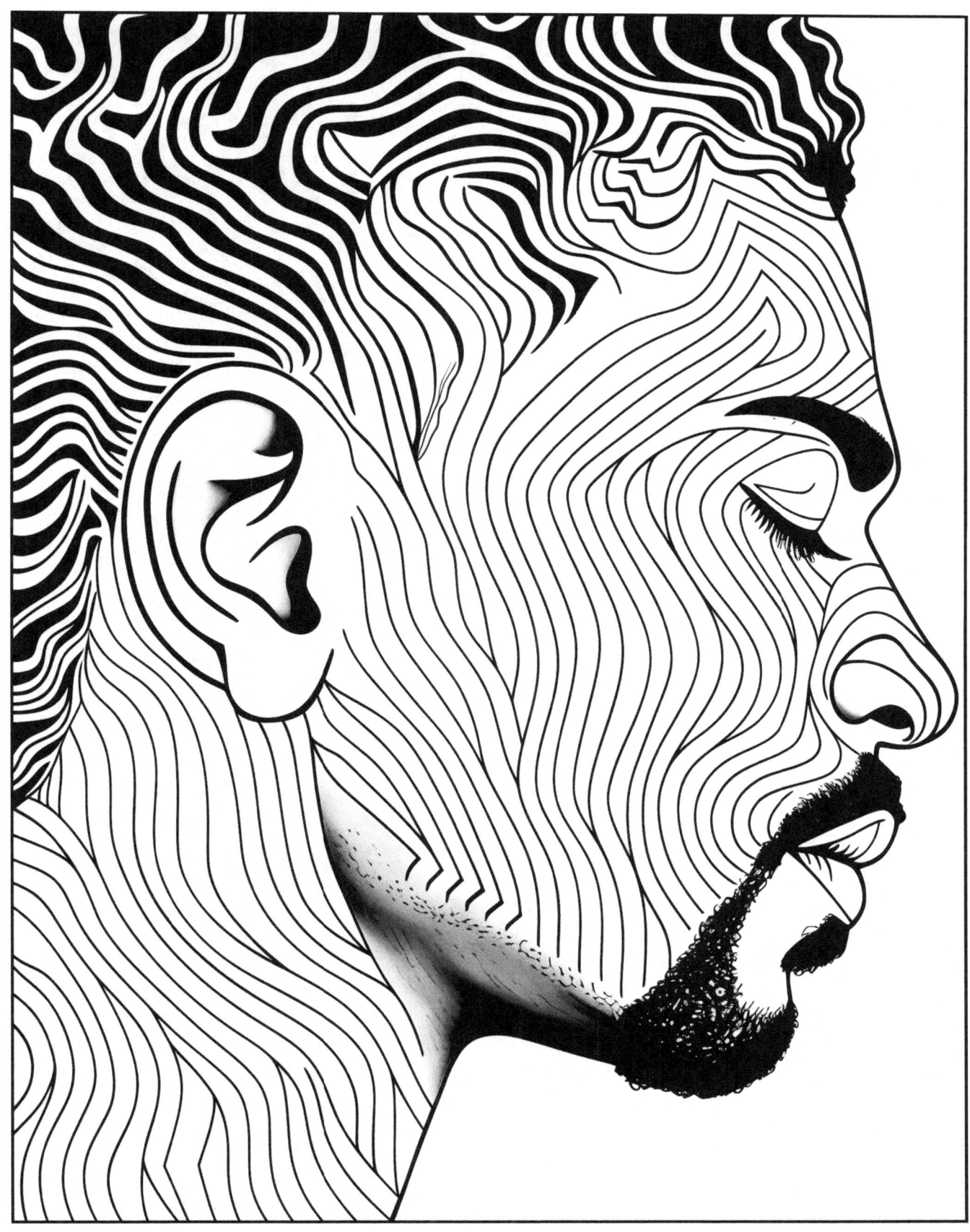

Contemplate the shades that bring you peace. With each stroke, think of a peaceful action you can take to leave a harmonious legacy.

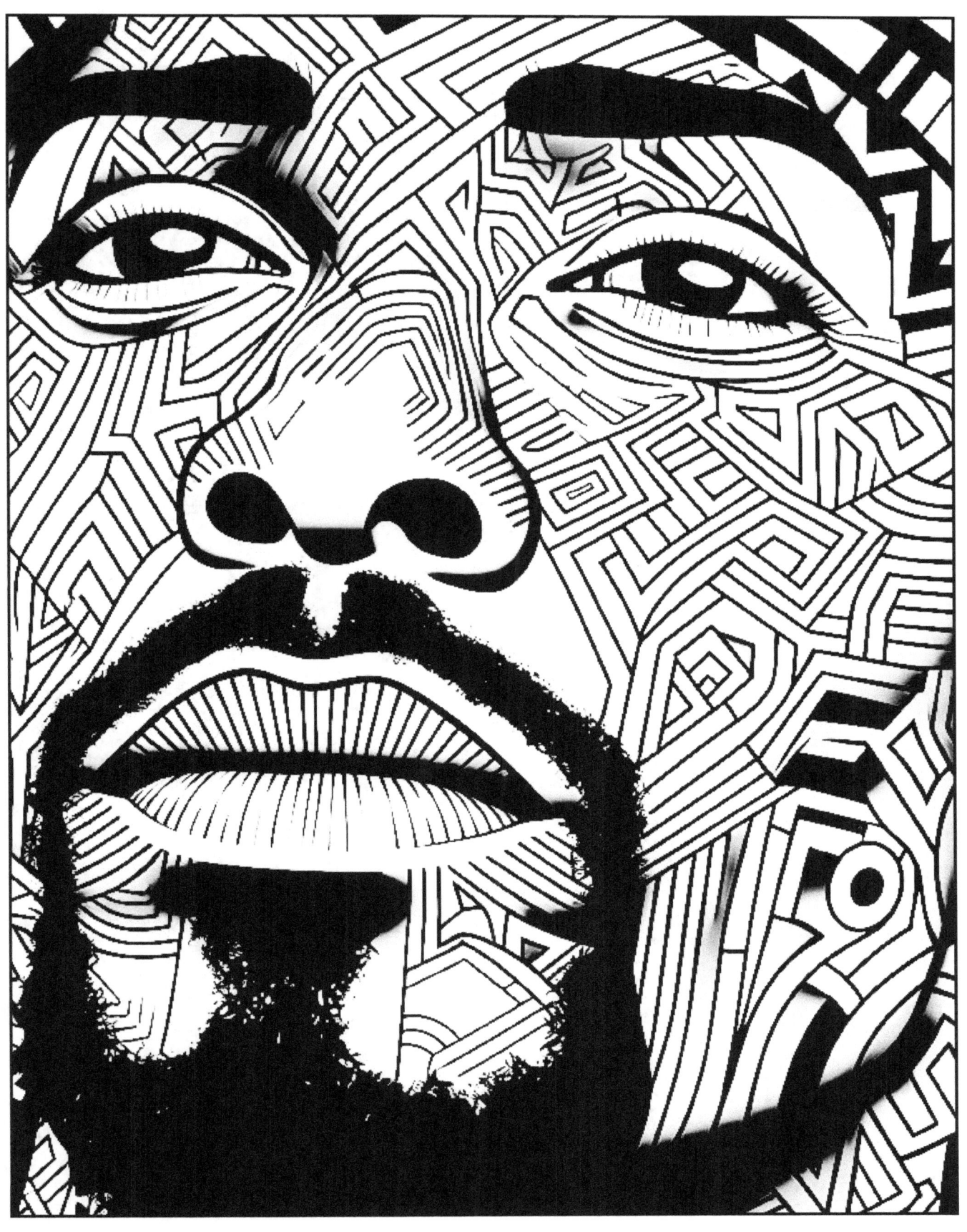

As you complete this coloring page, consider the completion of your life's work. What final picture do you wish to create, and how can you start painting that masterpiece today?

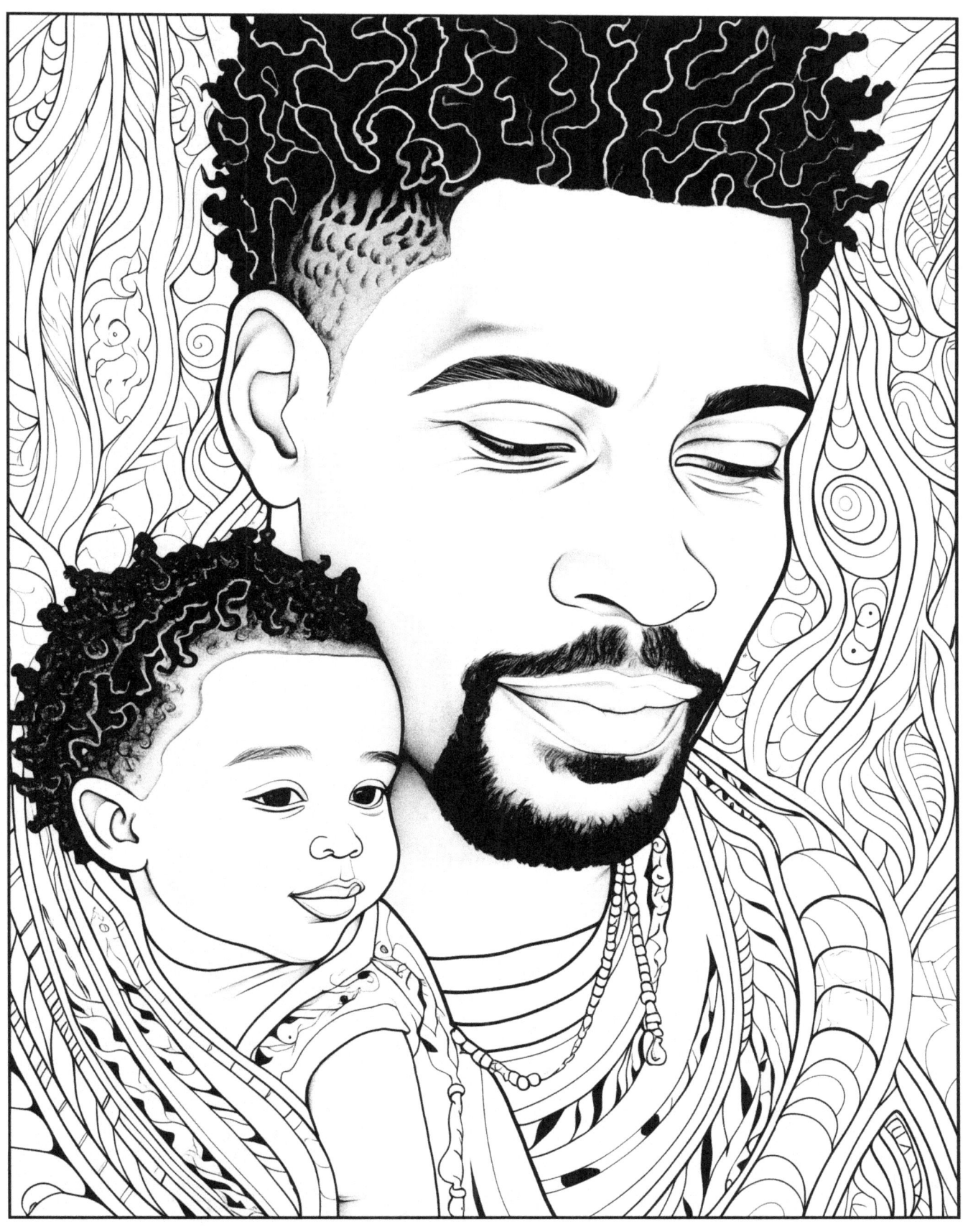

In the quiet moments of coloring, listen to the legacy of your heartbeat. What rhythms of life do you want to pass on?

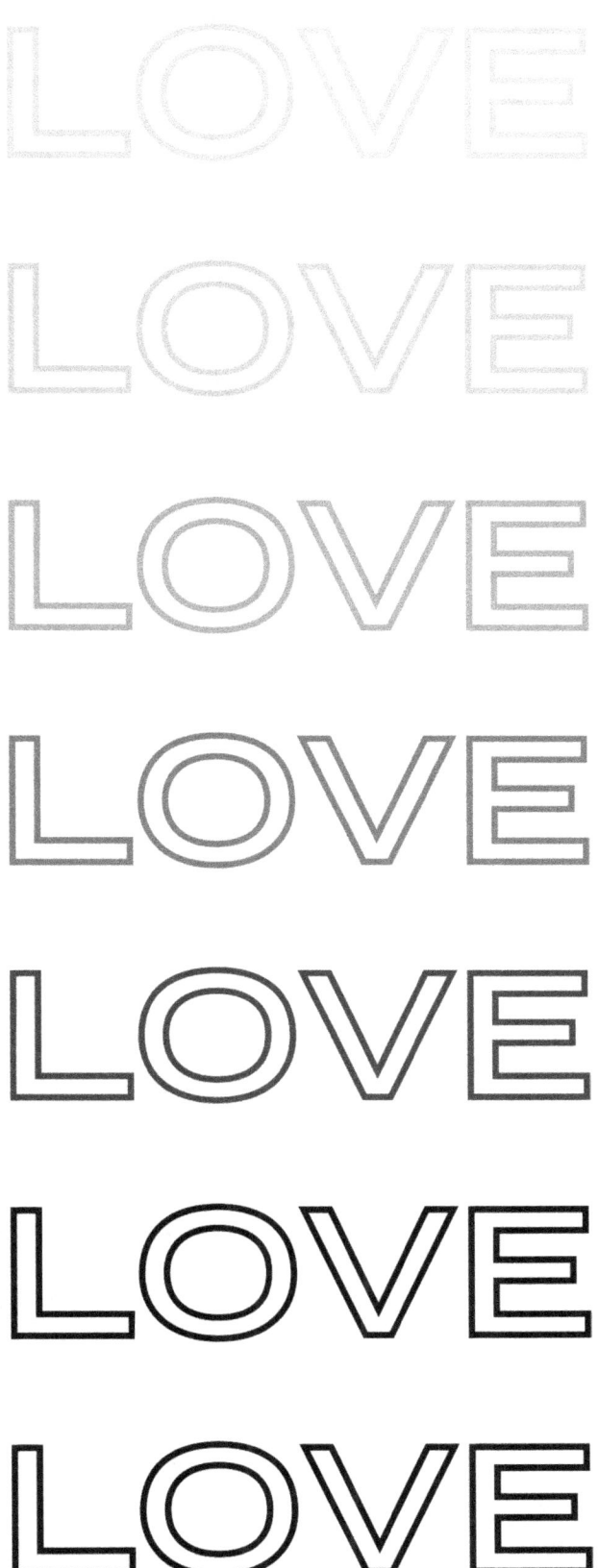

Each gesture and word influences a relationship over time. Envision how your relationship, with its unique joys and challenges, creates ripples that shape the future. As you color, celebrate romance, cherish how it evolves, endures, or reimagines itself.

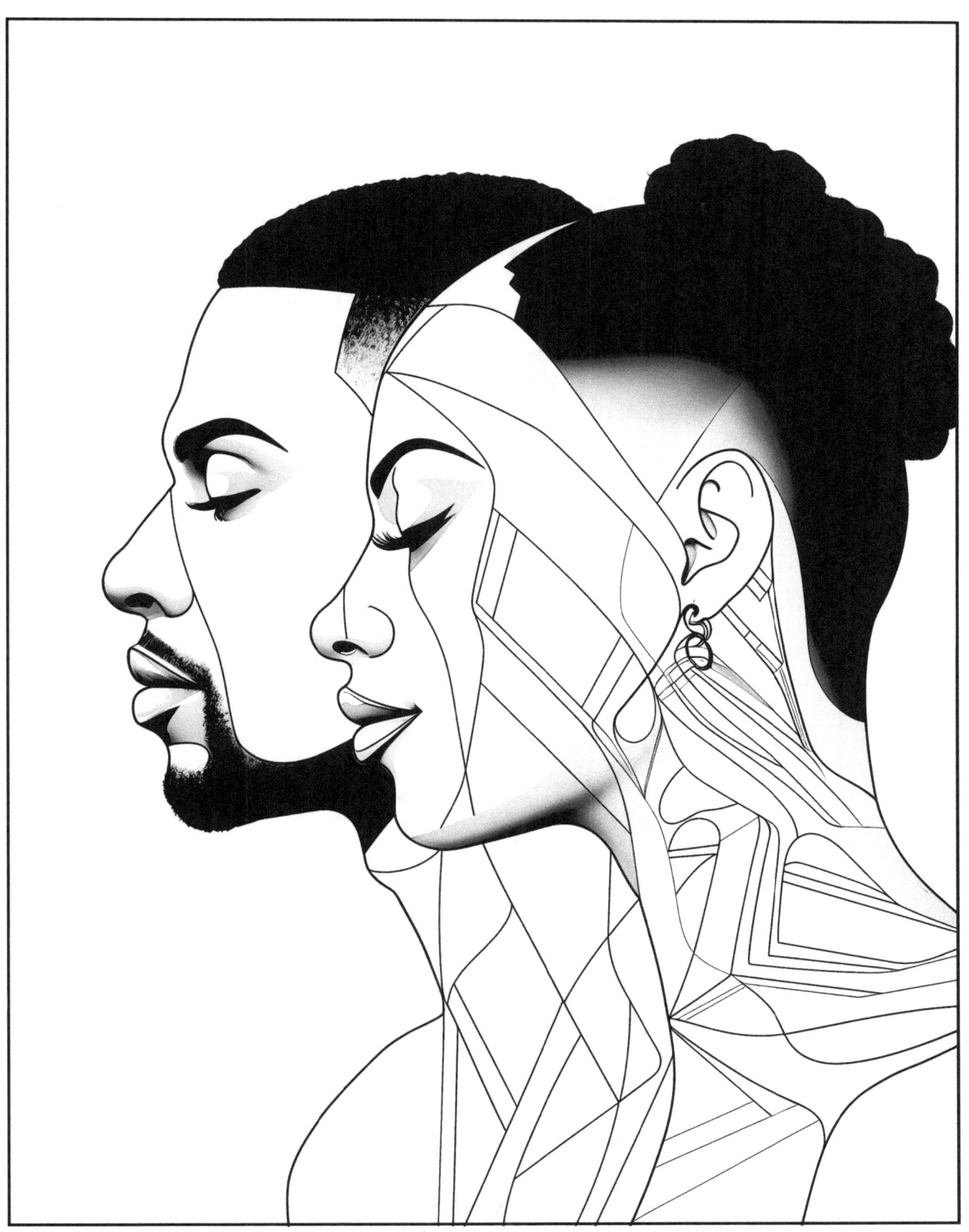

As you fill in the contours of their faces, ponder how your love has shaped and defined you both. How has your partner's love sculpted your life's journey?

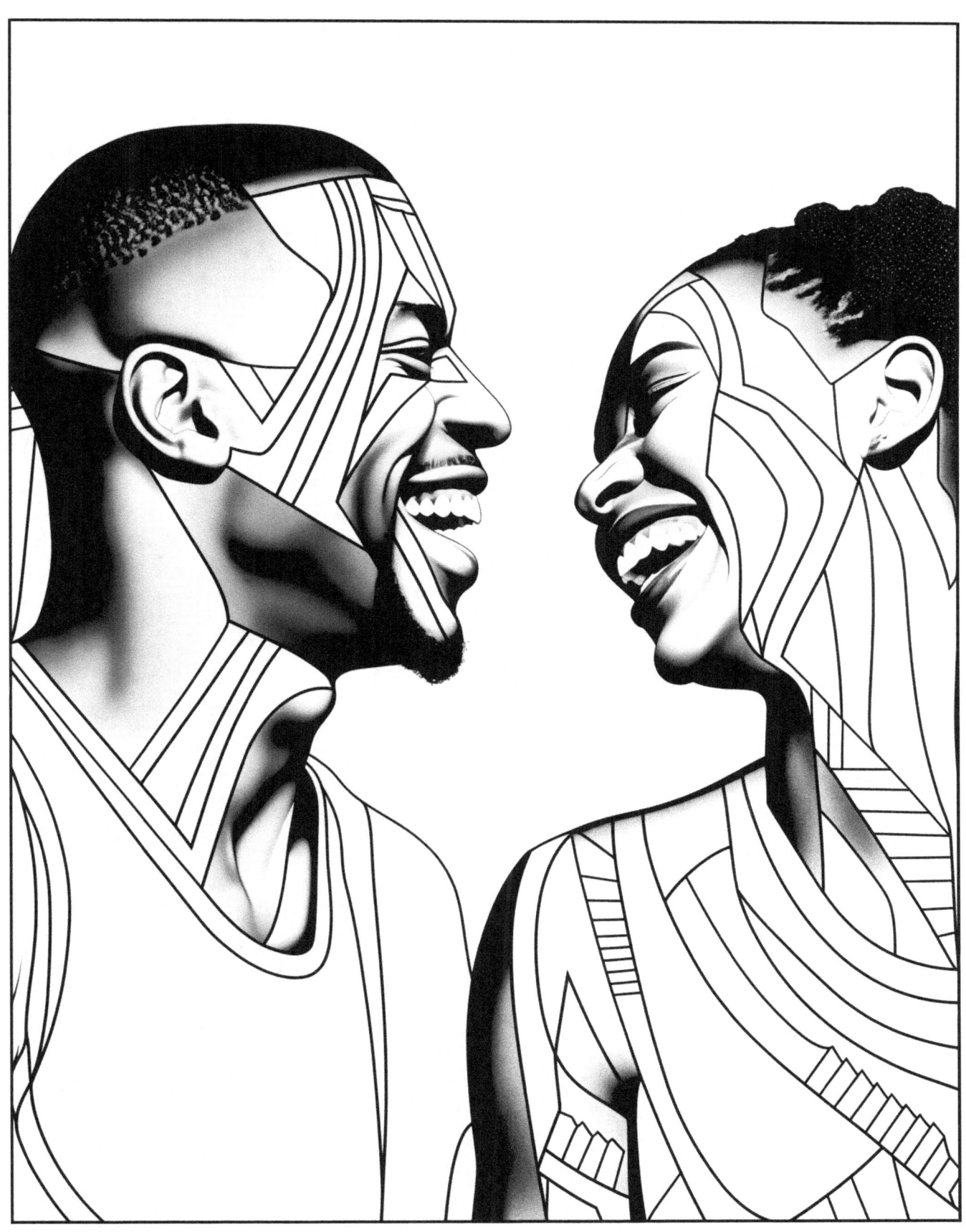

As you shade in joy, think about its place in your relationship. How can you spark more laughter—like attempting a gourmet meal together that ends up more like a 'meatloaf surprise' than anything else?

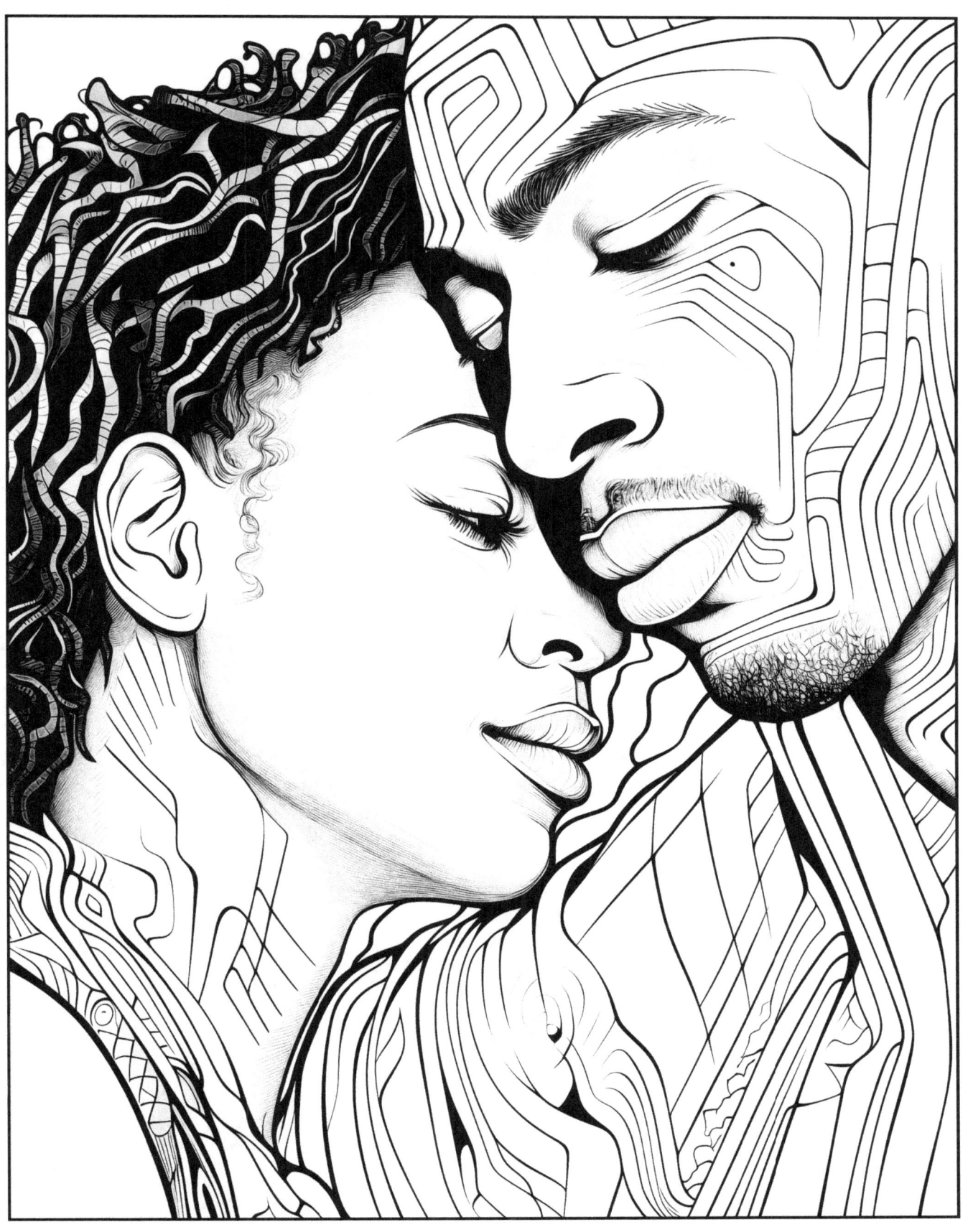

With each hue, think about the fresh starts. What new chapters are you both dreaming of? Maybe it's the simple joy of agreeing on a series to binge-watch together.

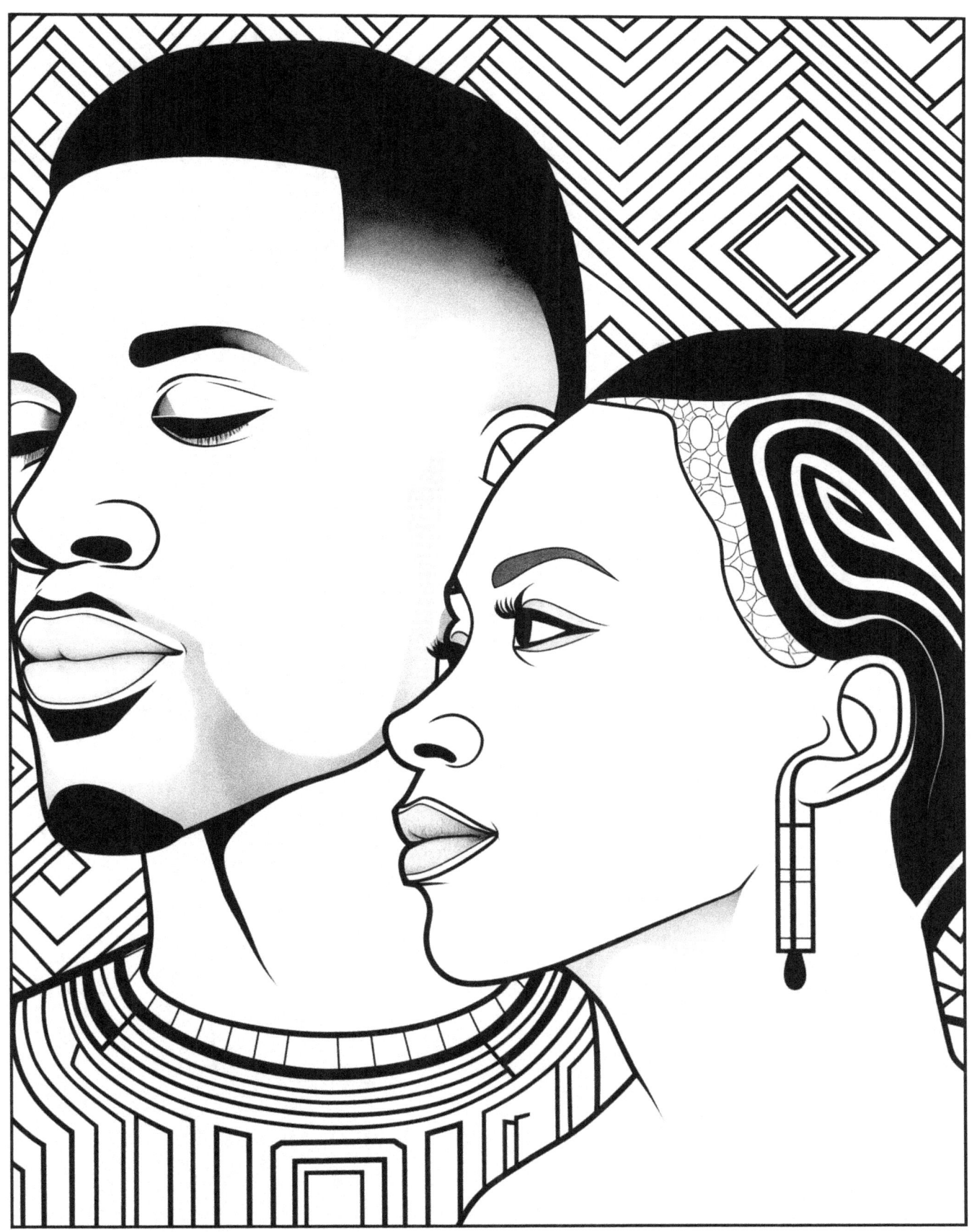

As you choose colors for the space around them, think about the environment you create for love to flourish. What can you both do to protect and nurture the space where your love lives?

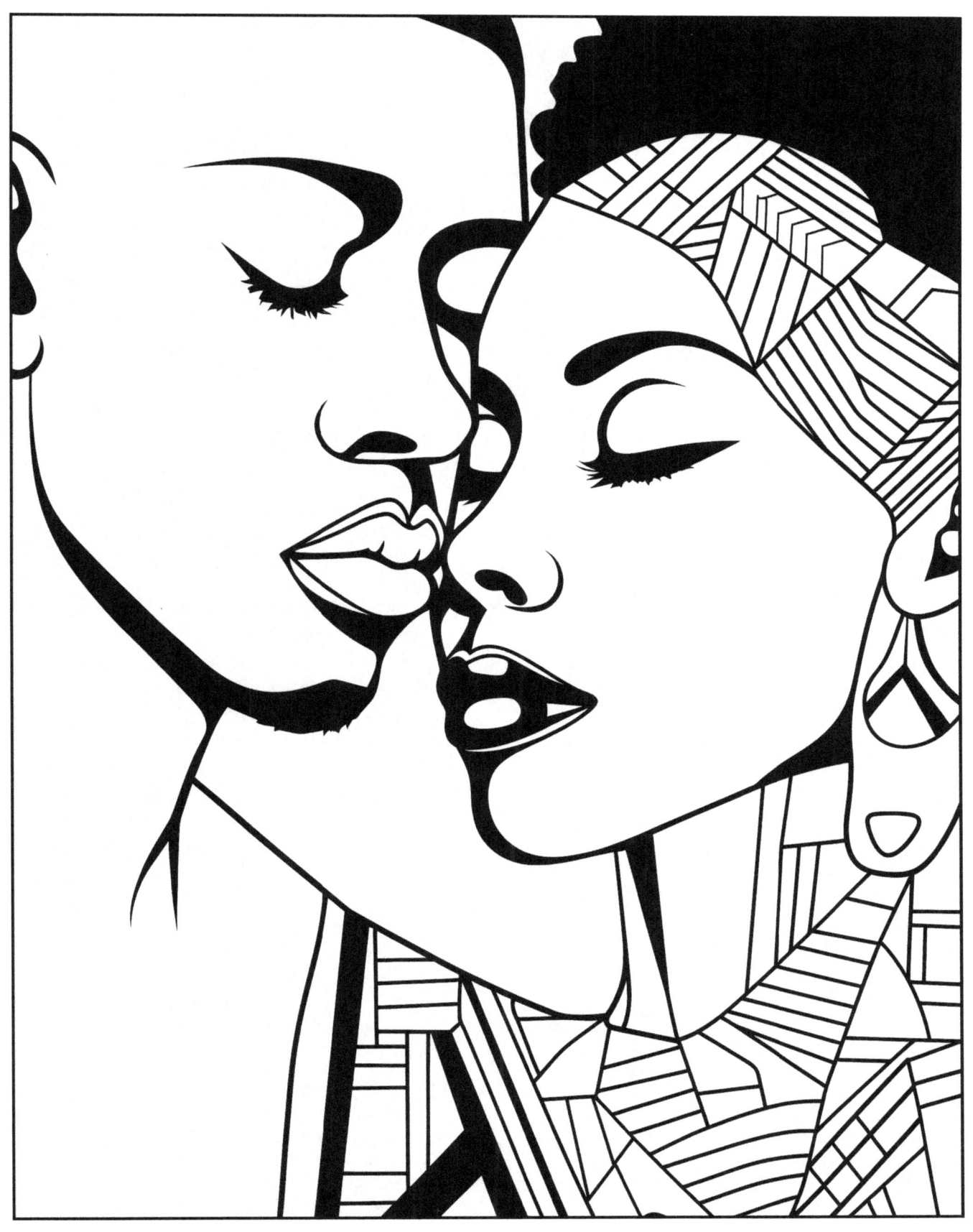

As you color these two, recall when your partner's touch brought comfort or joy. How can you communicate the warmth of that touch in your relationship today?

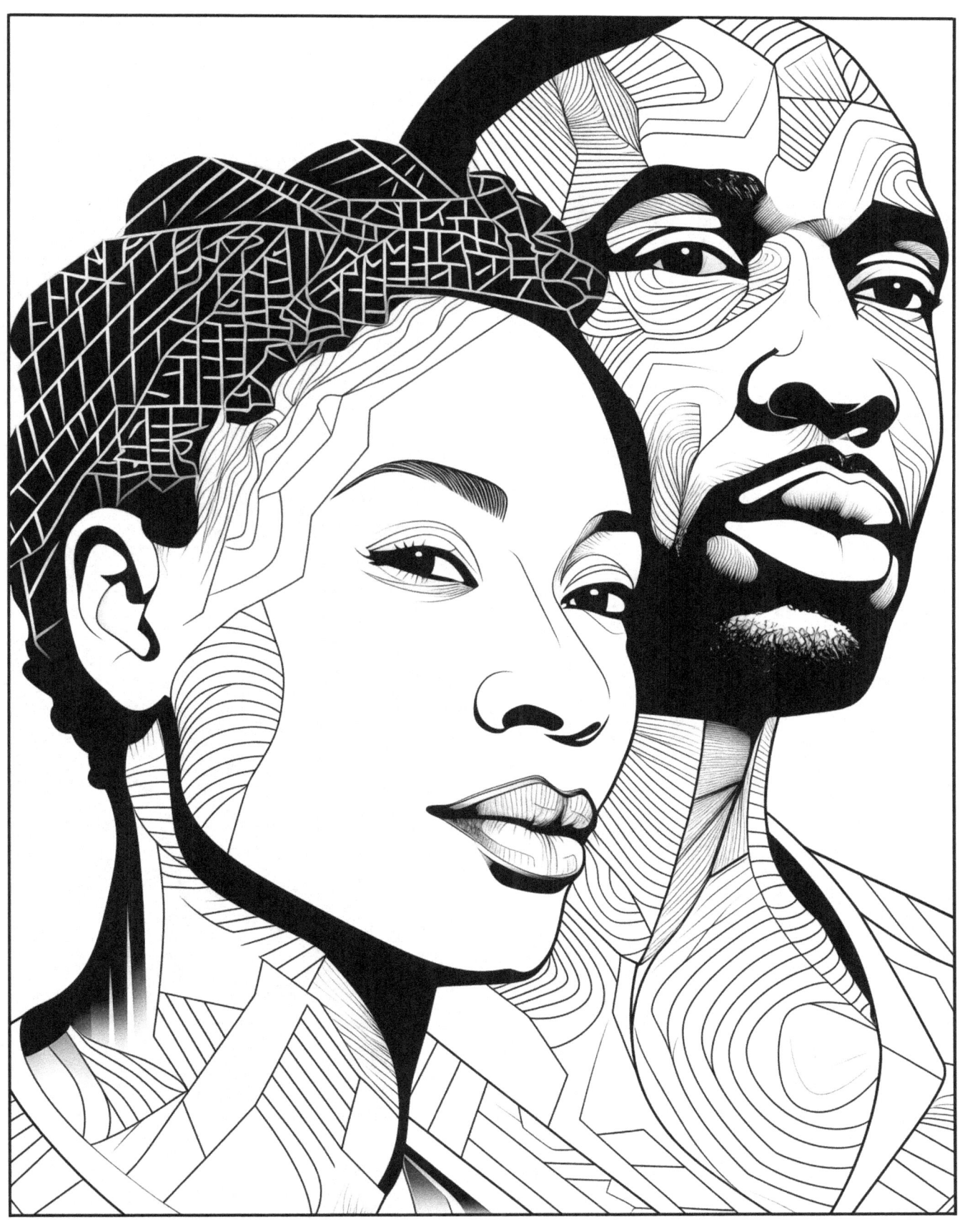

Reflect on the projects and dreams you're constructing with your partner. What is the foundation of your collective endeavors?

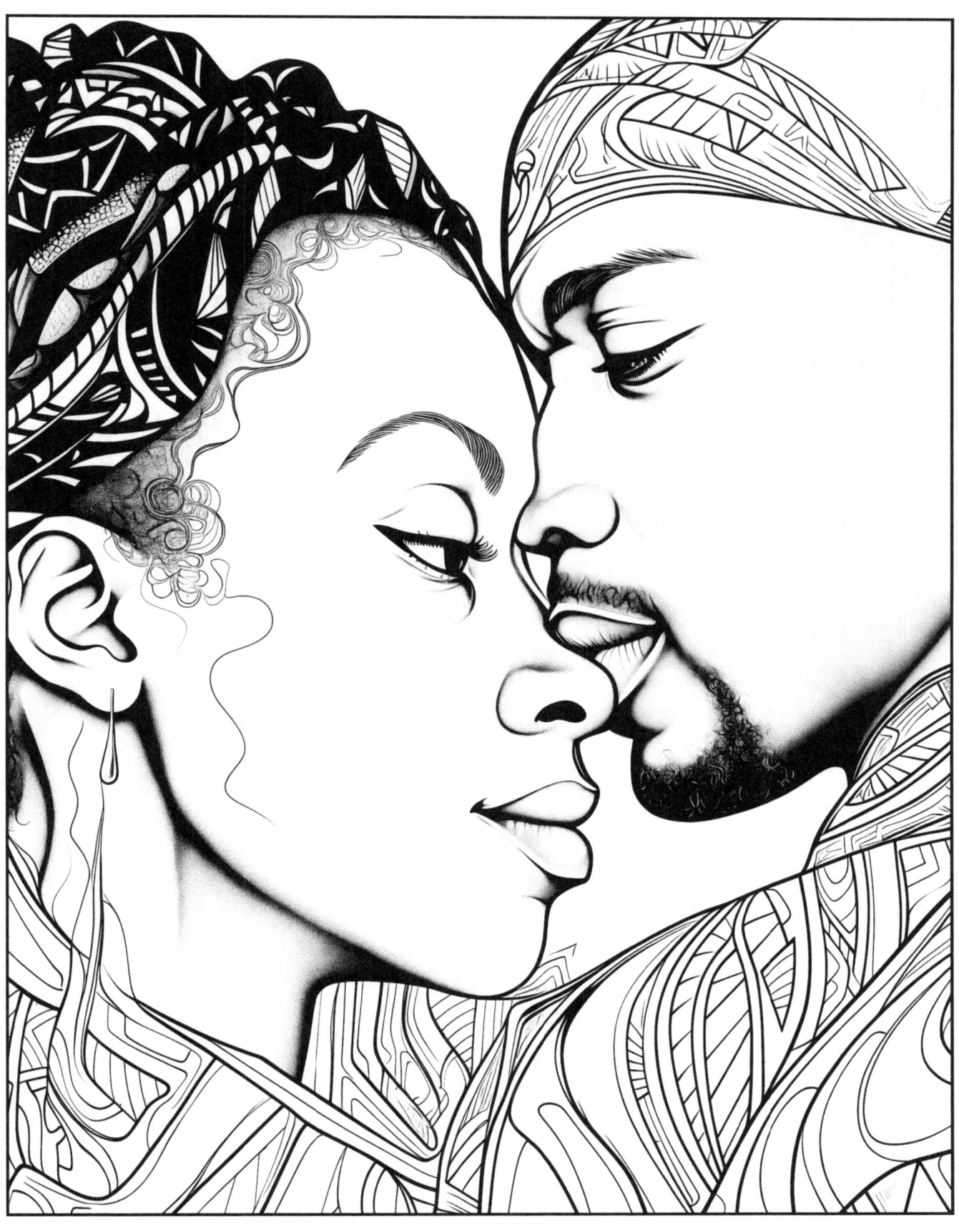

As you add color, think of a step you can take to walk in closer alignment with your partner's dreams and desires.

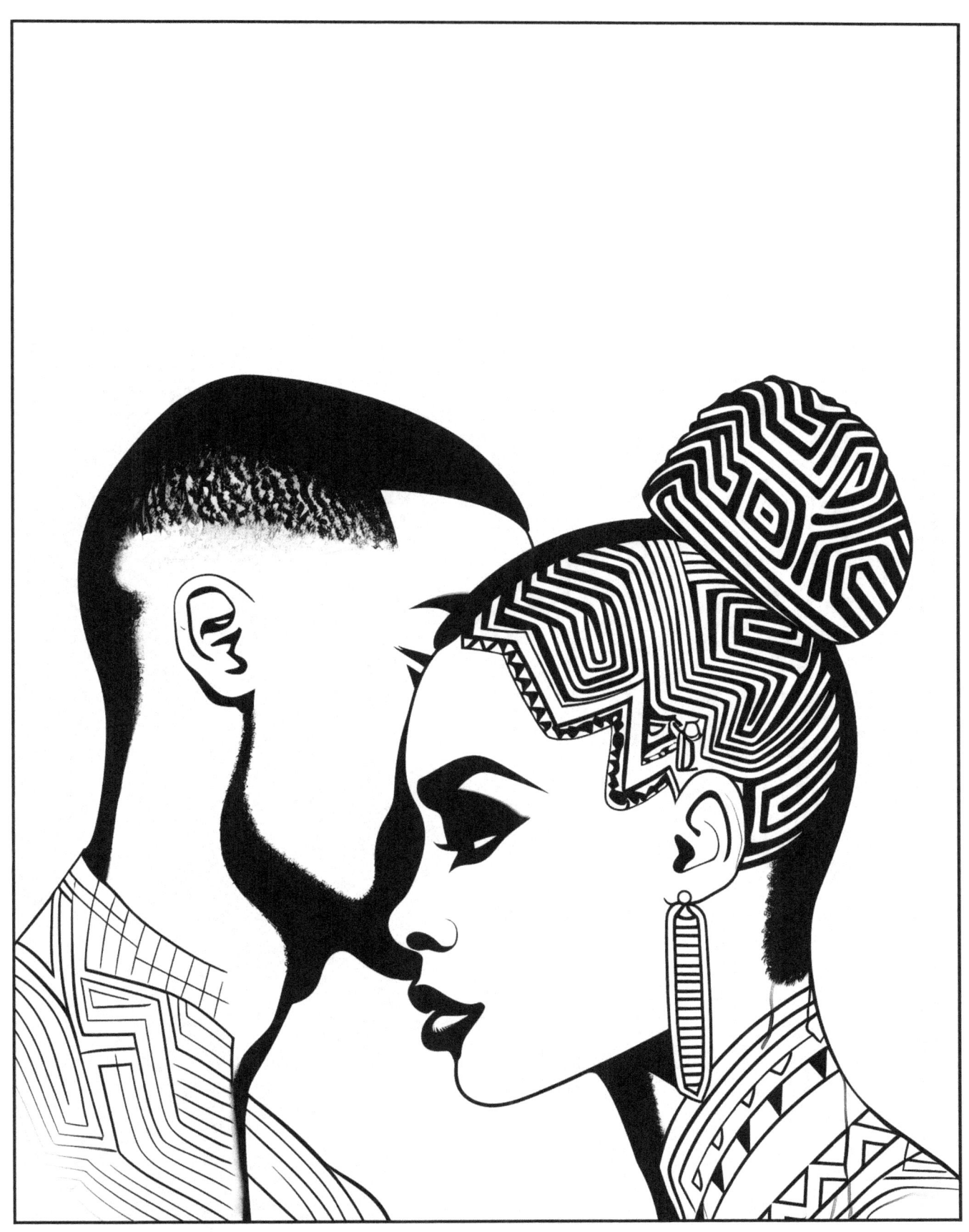

What words do you wish were spoken in your relationship? Or playfully, which ones would make for the sweetest apologies after stealing the last piece of chocolate?

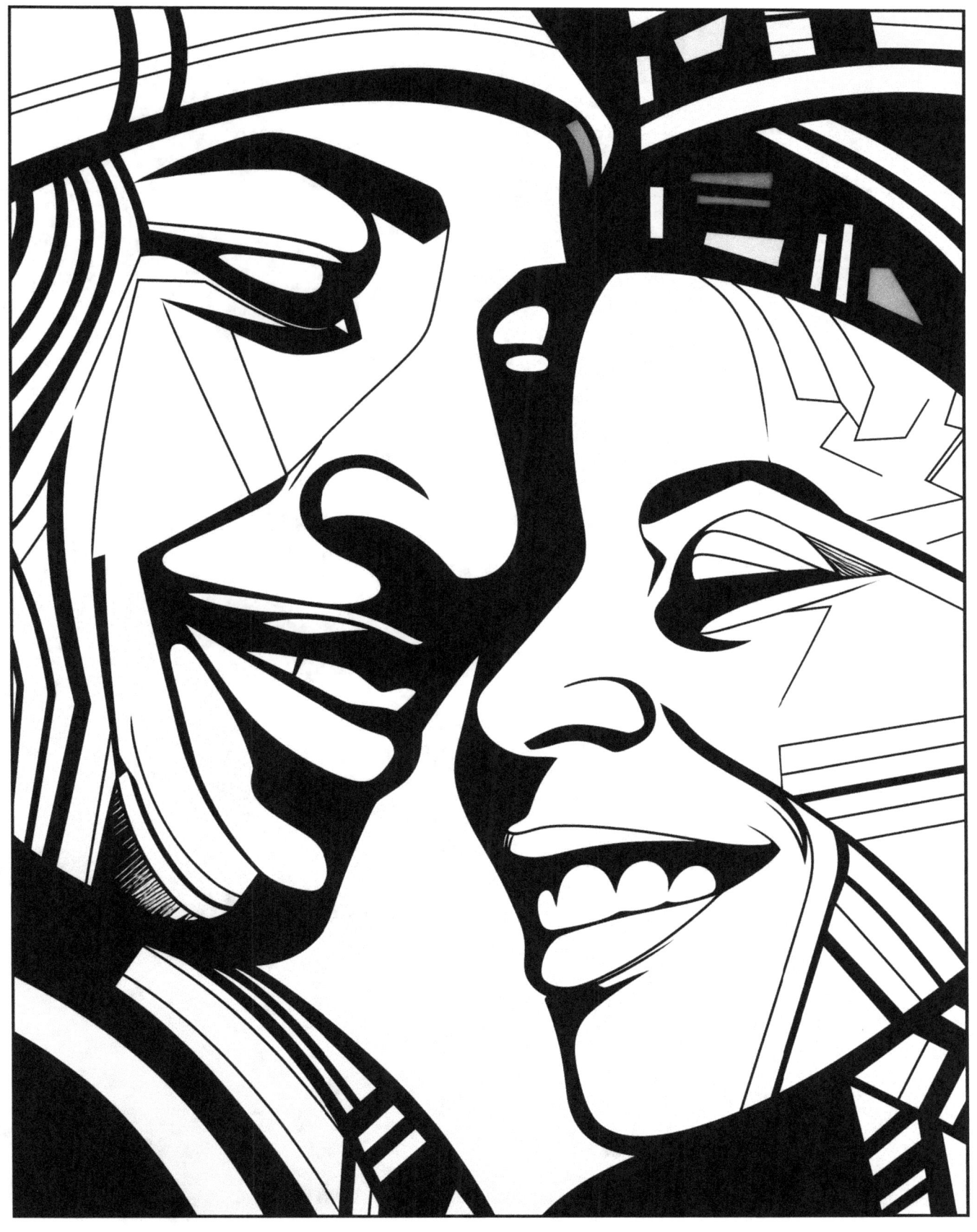

Think about the shelter you provide for each other. How can you strengthen the
sanctuary of your relationship?

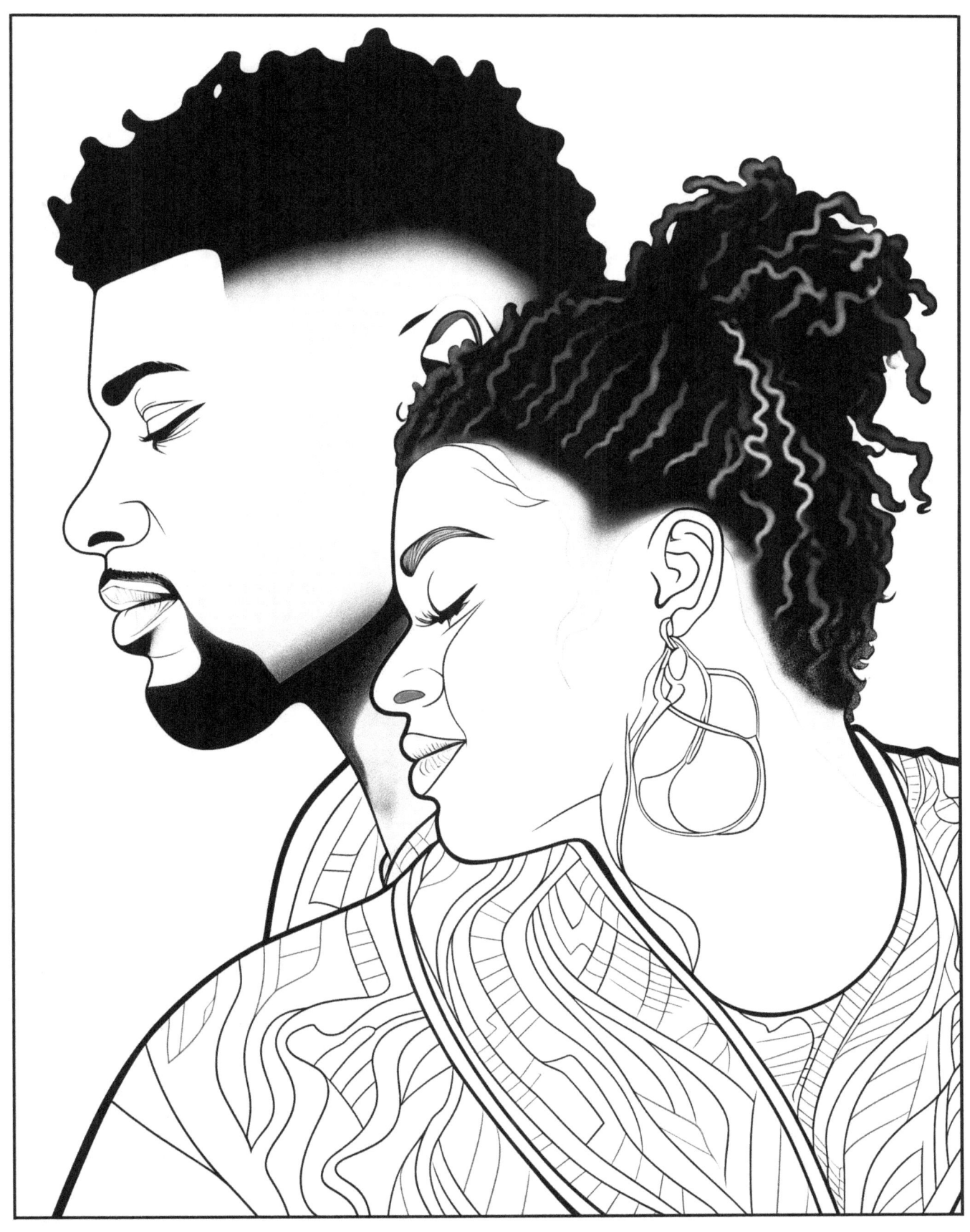

Let the act of coloring be a meditation on the power of closeness. What does it mean to give and receive support in your relationship?

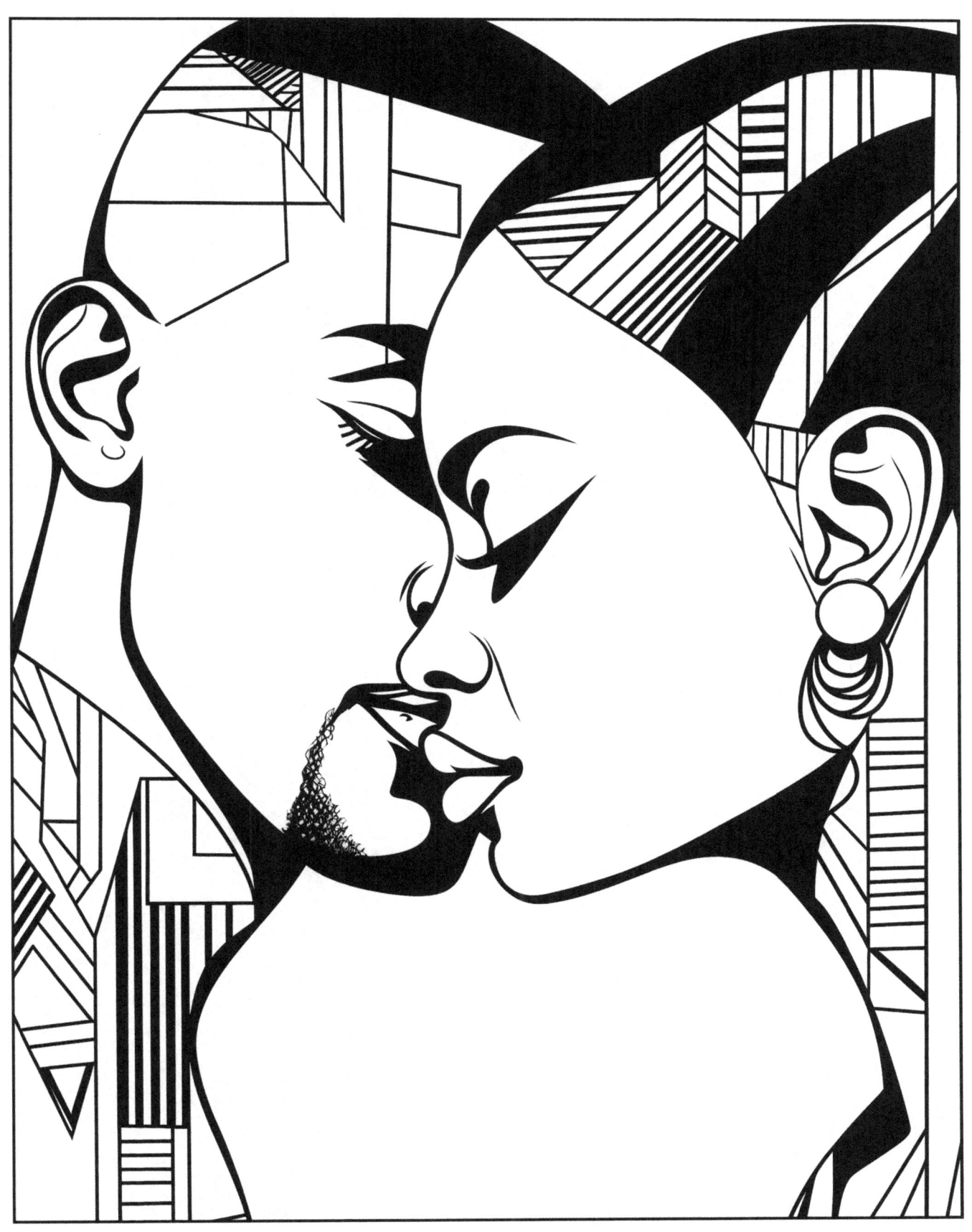

While shading in this couple, think about the unspoken understanding you have with your BAE. What silent messages would you like to convey?

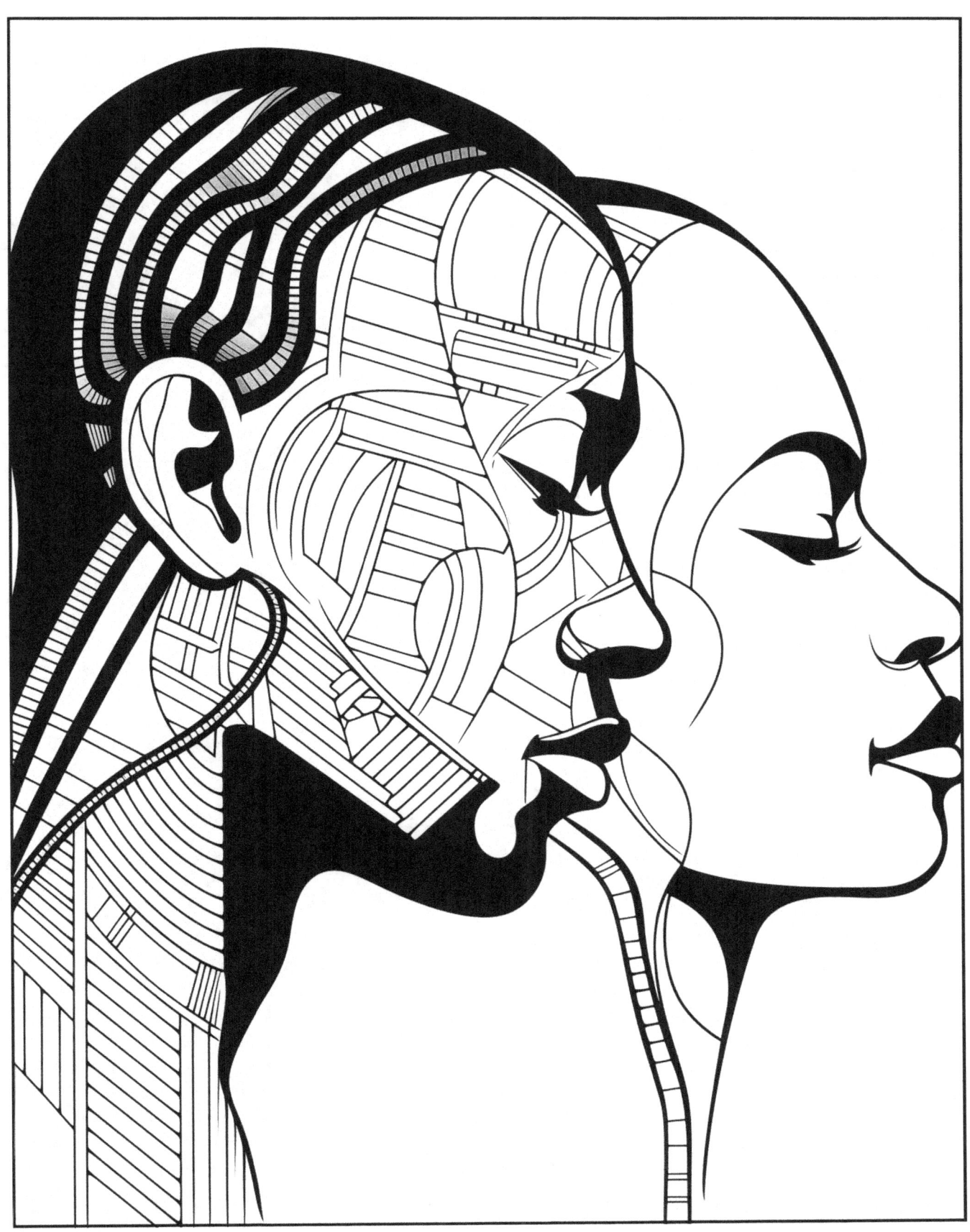

Color in the shared expressions of peace, and meditate on creating a tranquil and loving atmosphere at home—where even small victories, like the celebrated lowering of the toilet seat, contribute to domestic bliss.

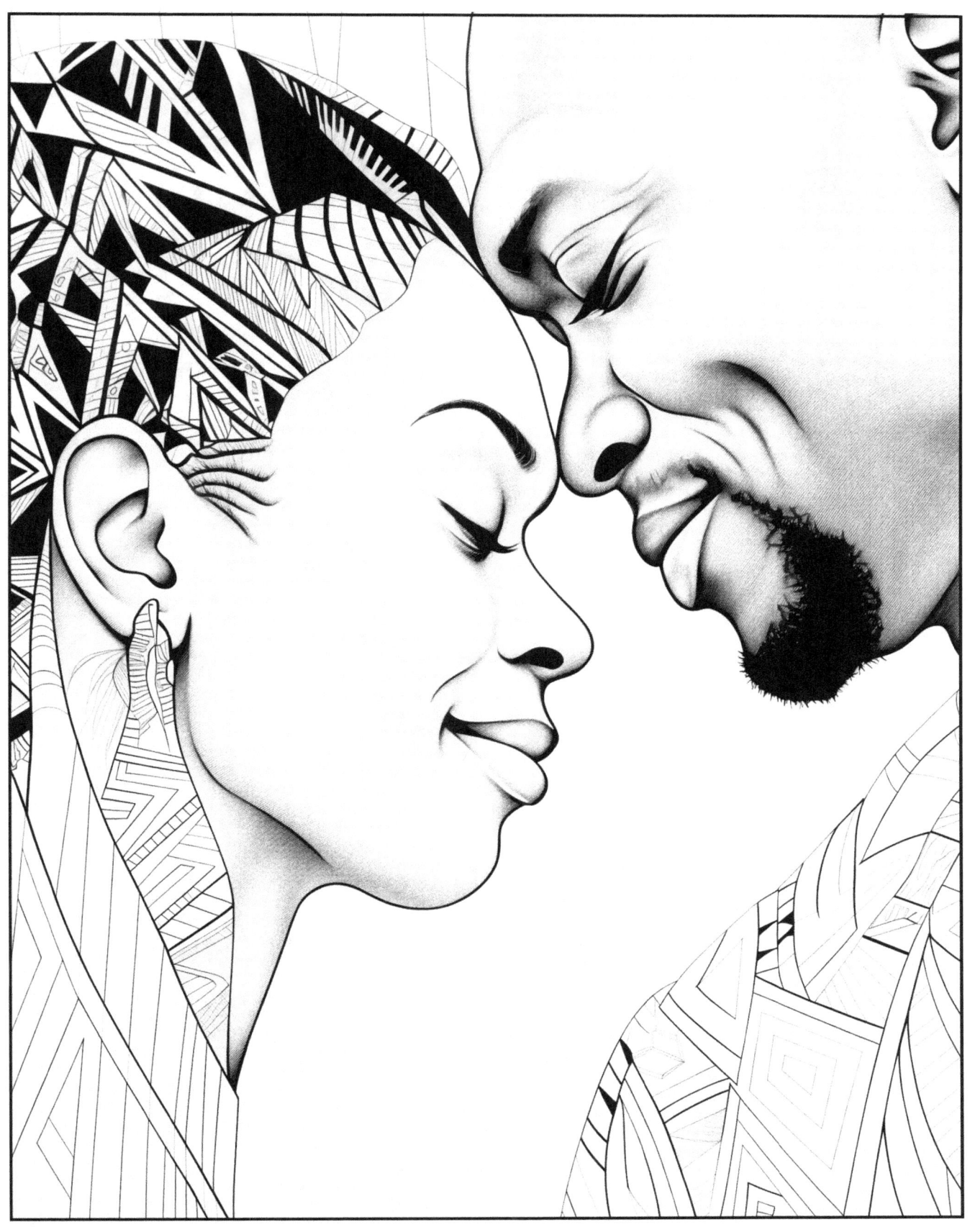

Fill this page with warm colors as you think about the ingredients of a nourishing relationship. What 'nutrients' does your partnership thrive on?

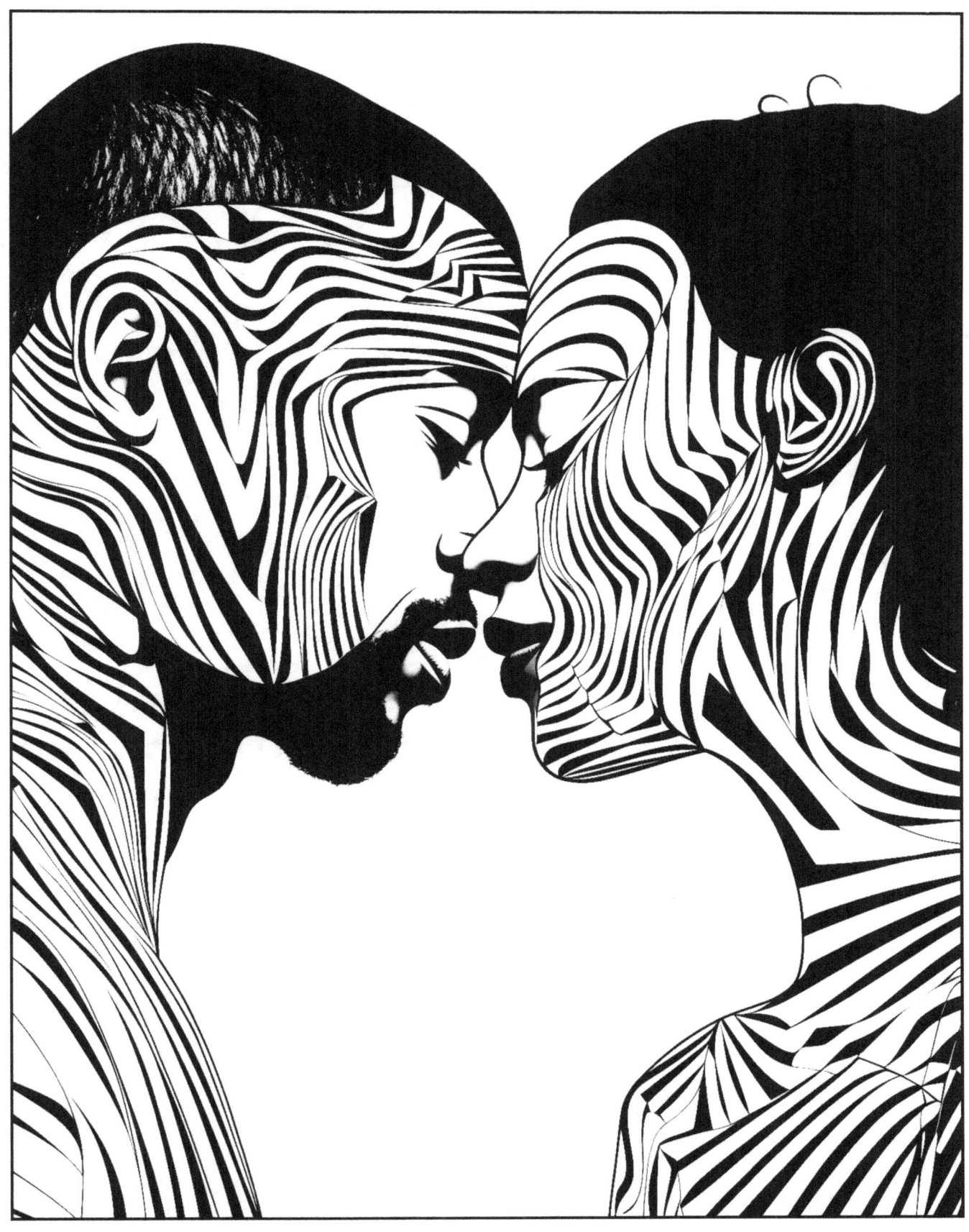

Color the balance of give and take in your partnership. Reflect on the art of sharing —perhaps by not just taking the remote but also offering the best seat on the couch.

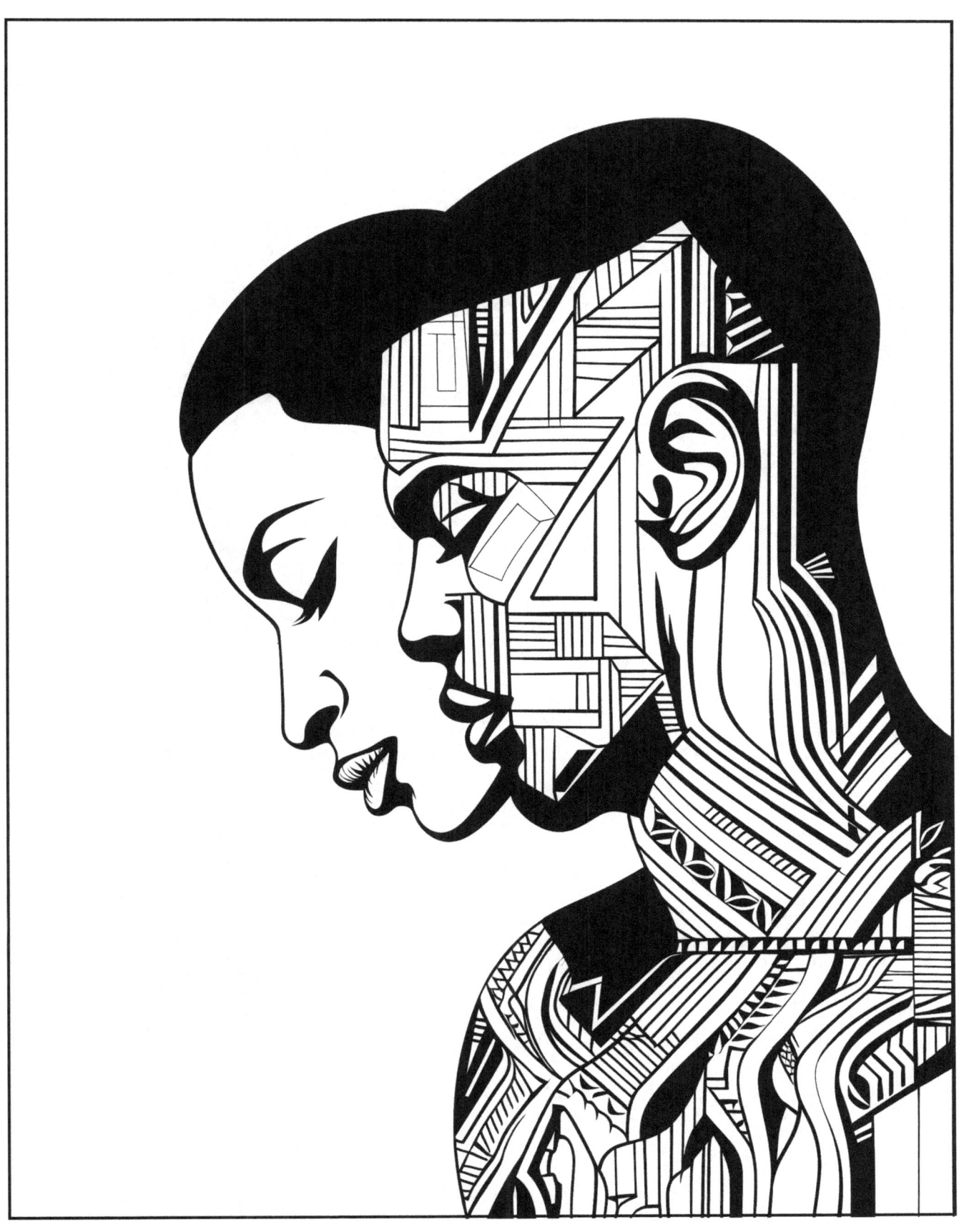

As you color this page, think about how your partner's strength complements your own—like how they might be the patient voice of reason when you're ready to assemble furniture without the instructions.

# *Acknowledgements*

Reflecting on this journey, my heart is filled with gratitude. The support and inspiration from those who influenced 'Meditative Men' has been invaluable. Their abbreviated names in the 'Acknowledgements' section signaled respect for their privacy.

With 'Legacy and Love,' my gratitude transcends the page. This volume is a tribute to every soul that has shaped this artistic venture—special thanks to Marukasa Teptah and Saamerikes Hetep for your insightful critiques that greatly enhanced this work. I'm deeply thankful to the Journey to Wealth - Women In Action community and the Authoring Affluence collective for your unwavering support.

To my readers and supporters, your embrace of 'Meditative Men' has deeply inspired me. The colorists and mindfulness practitioners, your enthusiasm is the bedrock of this journey. A heartfelt shoutout to the women who recognized this book's potential in nurturing young Black men with mindful practices - your advocacy is deeply cherished. Dr. Eve, thank you for endorsing 'Meditative Men;' your belief in its power for personal transformation is a great honor.

Your messages, reviews, and shares have not only spread the word but also affirmed the significance of fostering calm and connection. 'Legacy & Love' is crafted from the strong foundation you've helped establish.

To everyone who purchased, recommended, or found solace in these pages - your impact has been immense. May 'Legacy & Love' offer as much joy and reflection as you've brought into my life.

# About the Author

Harmony N. Soul is a passionate artist and craftsman dedicated to enriching lives through meditative and artistic experiences. With a keen eye for detail and a love for mindfulness practices, Harmony continues to experiment with this second volume in The Mediitative Men Collection, furthering her commitment to celebrate beauty and promote inner peace.

# Meditative Men
## Coloring for Calm & Connection

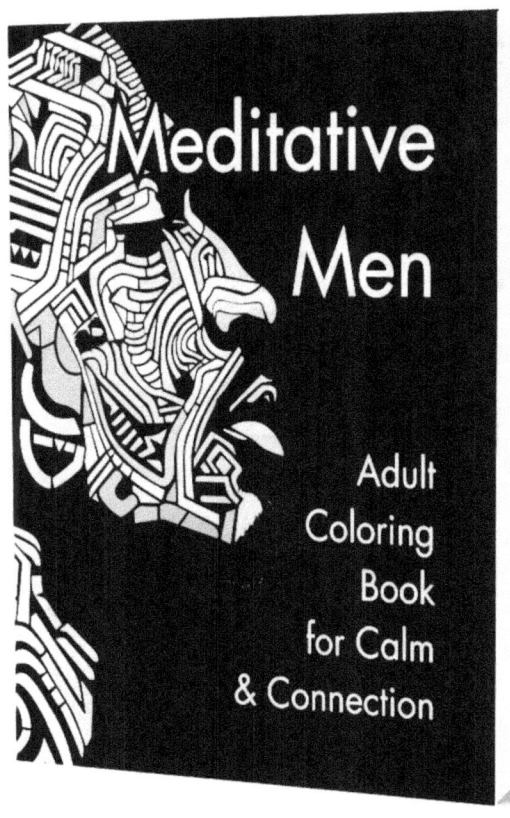

The twenty-five faces in Meditative Men serve as gateways to moments of calm and self-reflection. Each image was crafted to provide you with a pause from everyday life. Dive into Meditative Men to discover a deeper connection to yourself and the collective whole. Check out our rave reviews below!

**Top reviews from the United States**

Marie
5.0 out of 5 stars Love this coloring book!
Reviewed in the United States on October 25, 2023
Verified Purchase
I purchased the coloring book for my godson and now I plan to purchase for all the men in my family. It is such an affirming portrayal of Black Men that is so much needed today. The prompts makes the process thoughtful, meditative and insightful. The various portrayal of men is inviting. Love this coloring book! Looking forward to one for women and girls.

Amazon Customer
5.0 out of 5 stars moving meditation in color
Reviewed in the United States on October 6, 2023
This coloring book is unlike any I've seen in a remarkable and valuable way and its unusualness speaks to the need of its optics. The images are serenity inducing, as are the thoughtful captions/exercises. I particularly like that while there is continuity in the beauty and mysticism of each drawing and its heralded subject matter, each still offers a different pattern and design to make a creative and meditative practice out of. This book is absolutely beautiful!

https://a.co/d/hpCOeDP

SCAN to purchase

# What's Next?

Join us at
**www.meditativemenbook.com**
and continue the journey with
Harmony N. Soul. Discover
upcoming creations that promise
not only to inspire and delight
you but also to make every
moment you spend with us truly
worthwhile. Don't miss out on the
innovation that awaits—because
who likes wasted time?

www.ingramcontent.com/pod-product-compliance
Lightning Source LLC
Chambersburg PA
CBHW082144290526
45794CB00008B/3158